Illustrator:
Wendy Chang

Editor:
Evan D. Forbes, M.S. Ed.

Editor in Chief:
Sharon Coan, M.S. Ed.

Art Director:
Elayne Roberts

Associate Designer:
Denise Bauer

Cover Artist:
Susan Williams

Product Manager:
Phil Garcia

Imaging:
Richard Yslava
James Edward Grace

Acknowledgements:
Kid Pix®, Kid Pix 2®, and *Kid Pix Studio®* copyright Brøderbund Software, Inc., 1996. All rights reserved.

Apple the Apple Logo and Macintosh are trademarks of Apple Computer, Inc., registered in the United States and other countries.

Publishers:
Rachelle Cracchiolo, M.S. Ed.
Mary Dupuy Smith, M.S. Ed.

INTEGRATING TECHNOLOGY INTO THE CURRICULUM

PRIMARY

Authors:

Marsha Lifter, M.A., and Marian E. Adams

Teacher Created Materials

Teacher Created Materials, Inc.
P.O. Box 1040
Huntington Beach, CA 92647
ISBN-1-55734-933-9

TABLE OF CONTENTS

INTRODUCTION

Remember when technology in the primary classroom meant having a tape recorder? Maybe having technology meant that you were given the old typewriters from the office, when the secretaries got new typewriters. Times have changed and hopefully our primary classrooms have changed with them. "Why computers in the primary classroom?", you ask. "I have so much else to deal with." The computer is really just a tool and needs good software and a teacher who knows how to meld the software and the curriculum together. You will find that computers help students learn from each other, as well as develop a cooperative attitude in the classroom and lab. Computers can add enrichment to the content of lessons by adding an extra dimension. This book will help you to integrate technology into your own classroom curriculum.

Teachers have entered into the age of technology at all different levels, some teachers have been trained at their colleges, while some are having to learn at district in-services and college extension classes. It is our hope that *Integrating Technology into the Curriculum* will help teachers have a level playing field, whether they are new to technology or have been involved for a long time, and from this base, expand their technology horizons.

The first section of this book is devoted to an understanding of the hardware involved in using technology in the classroom, followed by a discussion of various computer configurations for classrooms and computer labs. You will even find blackline masters of a computer system that can be used to teach the parts of the computer and then made into a puzzle. Then you will find a discussion of the Internet and its uses for primary teachers , which includes some interesting educator sites and can be easily accessed. Finally, in this first section, you will find information on how to acquire funds for technology, in the discussion about grant writing.

The second section of this book has been devoted to lesson plans. These lesson plans provided will help you integrate technology into all the areas of the curriculum (i.e., language arts, math, social science, art, and science). You will find planning sheets, assessment forms, and even internet Web sites for many of the lesson plans. These lesson plans will help get you started on all of the different ways you can integrate technology into your current classroom curriculum.

The final section of this book addresses software. In it you will find a section on how to choose it. There is a listing of educational software catalogs that are available to you, and finally, a listing of primary software, each with a short description helping to figure out which ones will best serve your classroom needs. These software programs are arranged in subject categories for easy access. There is also a list of educational software dealers and their 800 numbers for your use.

Integrating Technology into the Curriculum is an excellent resource for classroom teachers looking for ways to use technology to extend their elementary curriculum.

WHAT IS HARDWARE?

Hardware, simply put, is any computer technology that one can touch. The computer, printer, monitor, keyboard, and mouse are all hardware components. These are the tools that carry out the instructions that the software gives them. Your brain, for instance, is the greatest piece of computer hardware known to man. It is a maze of interconnected circuits which carries out instructions that have been loaded through a lifetime of experience. What makes the brain such a perfect piece of hardware is that it is continually being upgraded to process faster and remember things better. Computer hardware, on the other hand, needs to be physically upgraded or even replaced periodically in order to run new or more powerful software.

Educators are faced with having to know what the capabilities of their hardware are in order to use it to its potential. This section will provide the background you need to determine the capabilities of different pieces of hardware. Each piece of hardware and its function are described, as well as tips on care and maintenance.

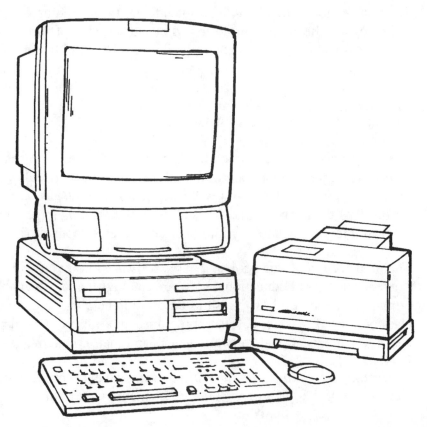

There are two computer blackline masters found on pages 23 and 24 that you can reproduce. One blackline master has the different parts labeled, and one does not. Have your students color in the blackline master with the names and then place the page in a folder where every student can look at his/her work whenever he/she wants. Have your students color in the second blackline master, cut out the different parts, label each one, and glue them on a separate piece of paper in the correct order. It should look like the computer system found on page 23. This project should help to familiarize your students with the different hardware pieces and their names.

The blackline master on page (23) can be used as a study guide, or you might use whiteout to mask the labels, duplicate the page, and have students label the hardware parts.

COMPUTERS

CHOOSING A COMPUTER

Much like choosing an automobile, choosing a computer can be a daunting task. There are several manufacturers that package computers in hundreds of ways. They use model numbers and slick names to steer us away from "what's under the hood."

PLATFORM

Platform refers to the type of computer/operating system that you require. There are two major choices: Windows or Macintosh (DOS ships standard on all IBM and compatibles). In the past, this was a major decision when considering a purchase in that IBM and compatible machines could not run Macintosh programs and vice versa. With the development of software translators and dual platform (they can run both) machines, the problem has become less significant. However, this is still a consideration. Here are a few questions that will help you or your school make the platform decision:

1. What platform is shared by the people with whom you most often share documents (office staff, fellow teachers, school sites)? If only one is used, choose that platform. If both are utilized, choose a platform that can easily operate in both environments.

2. What platform offers the software which you use or are interested in using? Most companies produce software versions for both platforms; however, because of the abundance of IBM compatibles, you will usually find them more accessible through retailers. Macintosh software, although available, tends to be easier to get through mail-order sources such as Mac Mall, Mac Warehouse, and educational suppliers.

PROCESSOR

The brain of any computer is its processor. The ability to handle large computing jobs with speed and accuracy depends largely on the processor. Computer manufacturers have evolved through several microprocessors, each generation fleeter and more powerful than the last. Don't focus on the name or model number of the microprocessor. Compare the speed of the processor with other models in your price range. The computing speed of a processor is listed in megahertz or MHz.

RAM

RAM or Random Access Memory is the computer's short-term memory which it needs to carry out a program's instructions. As software becomes more and more memory intensive, it is important to buy a computer with enough RAM to handle it. RAM's unit of measure is the megabyte or MB. Here are a few questions to ask when considering a purchase:

1. How much RAM does the operating system software use? Windows and MacOS require a large amount of RAM just to run the computer.

2. What types of programs am I going to run? Many graphic intensive programs like educational CD-ROMs require several megabytes of RAM to run. Look at the backs of software packages that you are interested in, check the minimum RAM requirements, and then add at least 25 percent more as a safety net.

COMPUTERS *(cont.)*

RAM *(cont.)*

3. Will you run more than one program at a time? If you are a first-time computer user, you may not think that you will; however, the time savings of being able to move information from one program to another is extremely useful. If so, add the minimum memory requirements for both programs together and add 25 percent for safety.

4. Is the RAM easily upgradable, and what is the maximum RAM upgradability? As computer programs are developed that require more memory, it is important that you are able to "keep up."

STORAGE

Storage is the amount of long-term memory that a computer can file or store. There are several storage devices on the market. Like RAM, storage is also measured in megabytes (MB) or gigabytes (GB). There are 1,000 megabytes in a gigabyte.   Almost all computers now come with an internal hard-disk drive and at least one removable disk drive. Both of these would be considered storage.

MONITOR

A monitor is the screen for the computer. Monitors are available in many sizes and configurations. If you are to take advantage of the multimedia (text, sound, animation, video, photographs, drawings, etc.) available in programs, you will need a good-quality monitor that supports at least 256 colors. Monitors that support thousands and millions of colors are also available. Be aware that high-end, large-screen monitors will require the addition of special parts called video cards installed into your computer.

PERIPHERALS

Peripherals are things that you add to your computer, such as printers, scanners, modems, video input cards, digital cameras, etc., that enhance what it can do. When shopping for peripherals, study the job that you want to do and the software you need to do it. Ask the following questions:

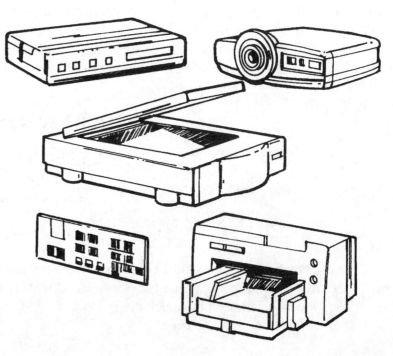

1. What quality are you expecting?

2. Will you need to add anything to the computer in order for the peripheral to work?

3. Does the peripheral require any software?

COMPUTERS *(cont.)*

IBM AND COMPATIBLES

In recent years, International Business Machines, Inc. (IBM) has made serious efforts to capture a portion of the educational market. Although schools still prefer the Apple platform, IBM and compatible computers are making their way into the schools more and more. The price and performance of IBM and compatibles make them an attractive alternative to Apple Macintosh.

Unlike Apple, IBM sold the right to manufacture computers that use their technology years ago. This opened up the personal computer market to "clones" and "compatibles." The added competition has driven down the price and increased the performance and quality of personal computers.

However, recently Apple has sold the rights to their technology to companies that want to clone the Macintosh. Begin watching for even bigger price wars as Apple tries to acquire a larger share of the personal computer market.

CLONES AND COMPATIBLES

There are a host of companies that have marketed their own versions of the IBM technology. IBM compatible computers can be seen in nearly every major electronic and department store, as well as mom-and-pop computer stores. Companies like Dell, AT&T, Packard Bell, Hewlett Packard, NEC, and Compaq compete with one another for their share of your computer-buying dollar. Each machine may have different "bells and whistles," but they all run using the same basic technology. It is important to assess your needs prior to choosing a make and model of computer for your school or home.

DOS (DISK OPERATING SYSTEM)

IBM's original operating system was DOS or Disk Operating System. It is, for lack of a better analogy, the computer's maid. DOS allows you to tell the computer where to store and retrieve things, how to organize itself, and how to clean up messes. It is a program that helps you run programs. This piece of software receives its instructions from the user through typed in commands. These commands are the code that users need to save, retrieve, or start programs. For instance, to run a program in DOS, the user might type something like this:

C:/PROGRAMNAME.EXE

Because using DOS requires learning a new language, as well as an understanding of the operating systems concept, these early machines were not user friendly. The mark against DOS is that it is user unfriendly. The operator must input a list of commands to carry out jobs that he/she wishes the computer to accomplish. Organization of files must be done by inputting a string of information on a command line. Newer versions of DOS have made this task easier; however, DOS still remains difficult for most to understand.

COMPUTERS *(cont.)*

MICROSOFT WINDOWS

Probably the most significant change in personal computer technology this decade was the production of *Windows* from the Microsoft Corporation. *Windows* provides the IBM and compatible user with an environment similar to the Macintosh operating system. The system is menu driven, with choices made by pointing and clicking a mouse, rather than inputting strings of commands. This operating system also allows the user to work on different programs simultaneously, easily exchanging text, graphics, and numbers from one application program to another.

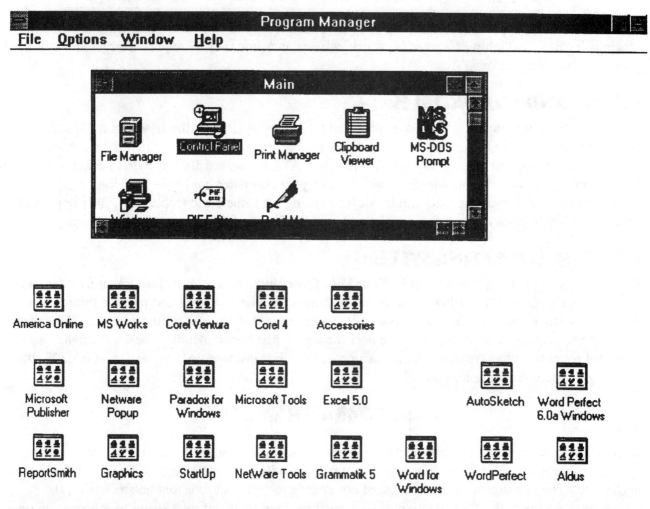

Microsoft Windows 3.1 © (Screen shot reprinted with permission from Microsoft Corporation)

MICROPROCESSORS

The brain of any computer is its microprocessor. The ability to handle large computing jobs with speed and accuracy depends largely on the microprocessor. IBM and compatibles have evolved through several microprocessors with each generation increasing in speed and power. Microprocessors are not the only consideration when looking for speed and power in an IBM or compatible; they are, however, good indicators.

COMPUTERS *(cont.)*

APPLE MACINTOSH: MACOS

With the advancements in personal computers came the graphic interface.   In the 1980s, Apple computer developed a computer and operating system that changed the way people thought of the tool. The Macintosh Operating System or MacOS uses graphics called icons to represent the files stored on the computer. Using an innovative piece of hardware called a mouse, the user was easily able to start, move, and organize files by simply manipulating the mouse. Apple continues to improve on the operating system.

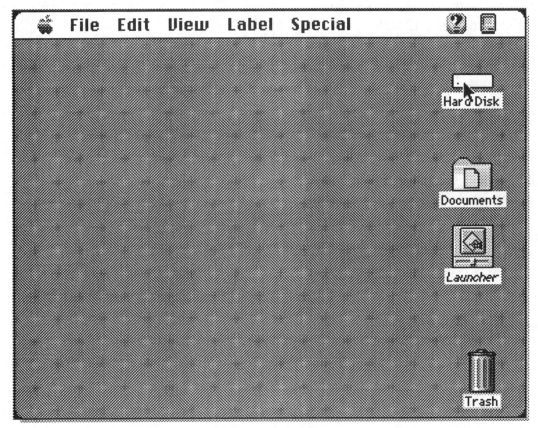

MacOS Desktop

MAC COMPATIBLES

As of 1995, several computer companies have begun to make Mac compatibles and clones. Like the IBM compatibles, these computers perform as well, if not better in some cases, as Apple's Macintosh. Some of the companies include Power Computing, UMAX, Daystar, and Radius.

MICROPROCESSORS

The brain of the Mac is much like that of the IBM and compatibles. It is continually changing. More speed and power come with each generation. When buying a Mac, concentrate on the speed of the processor, not the model number or name. These speeds are expressed in megahertz or MHz. The higher the number, the faster the machine. Remember that this is not the only benchmark of performance.

COMPUTERS *(cont.)*

MONITORS

The monitor is the screen that the user looks at when interacting with the computer.

Size

Monitors, like TVs, come in several different sizes. The measurement of a monitor is a straight diagonal line from corner to corner of the screen. Most home and school monitors are a 13"–15" (32.5 cm–38 cm) diagonal pictures. Prices of monitors over 15" (38 cm) increase rapidly and are usually overkill for student use unless used for school newspaper or yearbook layouts.

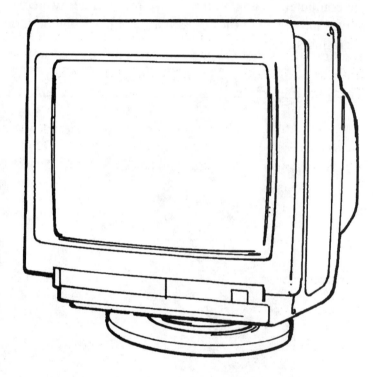

Resolution

The resolution of the picture refers to the number of tiny pixels (or lights) there are on a monitor screen. This is usually expressed in a number sentence that shows the dimensions of the screen in pixels (e.g., 640 x 480). The more pixels, the more true the picture is on the screen.

High-Resolution Video Cards

In order to display high-resolution computer images on larger monitors, you must have a high-resolution video card. The circuit board that is installed inside your computer contains VRAM or Video Random Access Memory. This memory is there solely for the purpose of allowing you to draw an image on the screen without slowing down your work.

Projecting on a TV

Displaying an image on a TV is a very good way to use the computer as a presentation tool. Whether using it to teach the class how to use a program or using it as a visual aid for a science lesson, it is advantageous to connect the computer to a television. Because computers are based on a high-resolution video signals, you cannot simply plug one into a TV. You must first use what is known as a print-to-video or video-conversion box to convert the high-resolution signal to a regular TV RF signal. Some examples are listed in the Large Screen Projection Section on page 16.

INPUT DEVICES

Input devices are those items that allow the user to interact with or input information into, the computer. Input devices include the keyboard, mouse, touch pad, trackball, graphics tablet, touchscreen, and microphone.

KEYBOARD

There are several keyboards on the market with a wide range of prices. Most fall into two categories: standard and extended. Standard keyboards are similar to most typewriter keyboards except for a few additional keys that are necessary to carry out extra functions that are assigned by the software. Extended keyboards add several other function keys, as well as a ten-key, calculator-type keypad. These are preferable, especially if math concepts are taught with the computer.

Many keyboard problems can be avoided by having students wash their hands prior to using them. To clean the keyboard, use a mild cleaner on a rag. Do not spray the cleaner directly on the keyboard. If a key is sticking, use a cleaning spray made for electronic components to remove the obstructing grime.

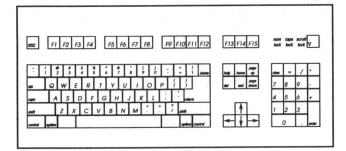 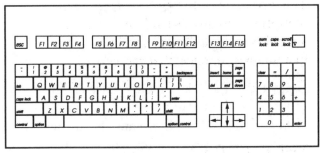

PORTABLE KEYBOARDS

Several manufacturers have developed portable keyboards that allow the student to enter and edit text, and then transfer it to a computer for formatting and printing. These relatively inexpensive machines are perfect for classrooms which do not have enough computers to allow the students enough keyboard time. For example, the student can write a story or report on the keyboard, do the preliminary editing, and then "dump" the text into the computer's word processor. From there the student can check spelling, format, add pictures, and print the document. Since the initial keyboarding is the most time consuming of these tasks, the portable keyboard saves precious computer time at a fraction of the cost of a computer. Other models even allow the user to connect directly to a printer, allowing a student to print out the text for editing prior to publishing with a computer.

INPUT DEVICES *(cont.)*

PORTABLE KEYBOARDS *(cont.)*

These keyboards require little user maintenance aside from cleaning. To avoid damaging connectors on cables that interface with the computer, pull gently at a right angle to the computer. Make these connections easily accessible, as they will need to be used quite often during a project.

MOUSE

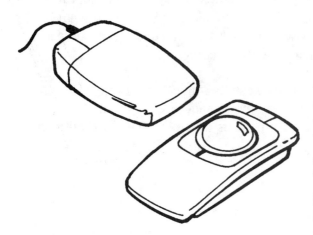

Named because of its resemblance to the rodent, the mouse is an input device that controls the cursor on the screen. The ball on the underside rolls against smooth gears which, in turn, send a signal to the computer and control the cursor. Mice come in several configurations, containing from one to three buttons. Once the user has the cursor where he/she wants it, the button or buttons on the top of the mouse can be clicked to move the cursor or select an item or items. The mouse works best on a mouse pad. Better mouse pads are made of dense foam rubber with a nonslide surface on the table side and a tightly woven cloth material on the side that comes in contact with the mouse.

Many times the gears in the mouse can become dirty or entangled with hair or fibers. To clean the mouse, turn it over and remove the ring that covers the rubber ball. Wash the rubber ball thoroughly with a mild soap. Remove any dirt or fiber from the gears with a cotton swab and a small amount of alcohol. Make sure that the ball is completely dry before replacing it in the mouse.

TOUCH PAD

A touch pad is a device that is an alternative to a mouse. Instead of rolling a mouse around, the user moves the tip of his/her finger on the surface of the pad. The cursor reacts much as it does with a mouse. A touch pad needs to be cleaned periodically with a mild soapy solution. Again, this should be applied conservatively to a soft cloth and never sprayed directly on the pad.

INPUT DEVICES *(cont.)*

GRAPHICS TABLET

A graphics tablet is a device that allows the user to draw freehand on it while it duplicates the drawing on the computer screen. Aside from the use in a graphics environment, this type of device comes in handy when teachers are presenting by using the computer. For instance, if a picture is shown on the computer or large-screen projection device, the teacher can use the tablet to circle or make notes right on the screen. Sports commentators use these same devices to call attention to details on a replay by drawing directly on the screen.

Care of a graphics tablet is much the same as for a touch pad. Keeping the tablet clean will enhance its performance and extend its life.

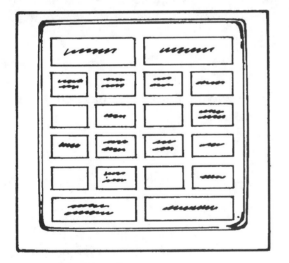

TOUCHSCREEN

Very useful for special needs children who have underdeveloped fine motor coordination, the touchscreen is an overlay to the monitor. When accompanied with the appropriate software, users touch the screen to make the selection they require in a program. These are used in informational kiosks (e.g., wedding registers at major department stores).

Once again, keeping the touchscreen clean by dusting and wiping with a slightly damp cloth will help to avoid problems.

MICROPHONES

With the proliferation of multimedia computers and the use of recorded sound, the ability to record oneself on the computer has evolved. In addition, many new computers have a voice recognition capability. Many computers have microphones built in to do this, although the quality and flexibility of these is not usually very good. Several electronics stores sell microphones for as little as five dollars. Any of these will work as long as the plug is the right size. Most computers accept the 1/8 inch miniplug.

Take care not to bump the plug while it is in the socket of the computer, as that can cause the socket to be damaged or shear off the plug. Again, occasionally cleaning the microphone will assure that it lasts a long time.

OUTPUT DEVICES

AV INPUT/OUTPUT CARDS

Some computers are equipped with, or can have installed, AV cards. These circuit boards allow the connection of audio and video equipment such as VCRs, video cameras, laserdisc players, audio CD players, and tape recorders. When connected to appropriate equipment and running appropriate software, these AV cards can record audio and video clips for use in multimedia presentations by students or teachers. If the card has an output capability, the computer can be linked directly to a TV, VCR, or tape recorder. Computer sounds and images can then be viewed or recorded. This eliminates the need for a separate print-to-video box.

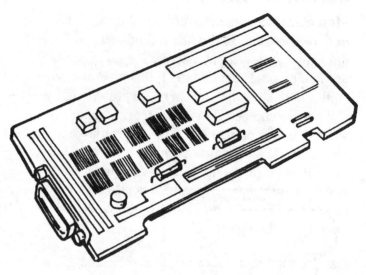

Since these are inside the computer, the only maintenance required would be the occasional (one to three times a year, depending on the amount of dust in the environment) cleaning of the computer's circuit boards.

OUTPUT DEVICES

Output devices are mechanisms that allow you to receive some type of product from a computer. Some output devices are printers, large screen projectors, and speakers.

PRINTERS

There are several brands of printers on the market. However, there are only three types of printers most commonly found in schools: dot matrix, ink jet, and laser.

DOT MATRIX PRINTERS

Dot matrix printers are characterized by very fast printing at a lower visual quality than other printers. A dense grid of metal pins impact against an ink ribbon to form the shapes of letters and symbols. It takes several pins to make the shape of a letter. Most of these printers are equipped with tractor and friction feed. Tractor feed requires a continuous roll of special paper with holes on either side that engage in the gears of the printer for advancement. Friction feed means that the paper can be fed through the printer by friction, much like a typewriter.

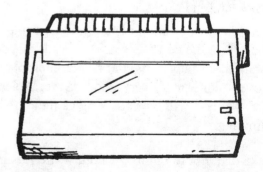

OUTPUT DEVICES *(cont.)*

DOT MATRIX PRINTERS *(cont.)*

Most care and upkeep involves changing ribbons and keeping the platen (rubber cylinder) clean. It is very important to keep continuous-feed paper free of obstruction so that tangling does not occur. Do not allow the printer to work without paper. Printing directly on the platen can cause damage to the dot matrix pins.

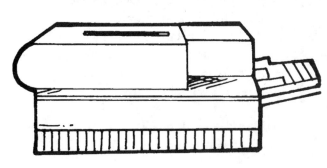

INK-JET PRINTERS

Ink-jet printers are very popular because of their flexibility. Although slower than dot matrix, ink-jet printers can print text and pictures in shades of gray and, with some models, even in color. These printers work by spraying ink through very small jets in order to form the shapes and shades required. Color ink jets combine layers of red, green, and blue to achieve different hues and shades.

Maintenance includes the changing of the ink cartridge and the occasional cleaning of metal contacts and the jets themselves. Many models are self-cleaning, eliminating the bother of a cleaning ritual. Avoiding low-quality paper will result in a better quality of print job and a longer time period between cleaning.

LASER PRINTERS

Laser printers work much like photocopiers. A thin layer of toner powder is distributed over the surface of the paper. A laser draws the shapes and increases or decreases the intensity of the light in order to achieve shading. The toner, which is hit by the laser, adheres to the paper, and the rest is removed.

Once again, the quality of the paper and toner are important to the operation of the printer. Avoid contamination of either the toner or the paper tray. Keep the machine clean and avoid severe temperature fluctuations.

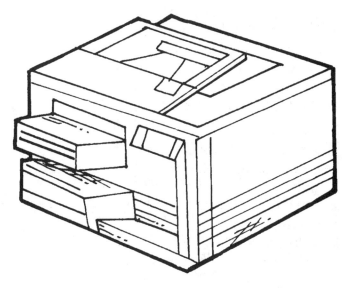

OUTPUT DEVICES *(cont.)*

LARGE-SCREEN PROJECTION DEVICES

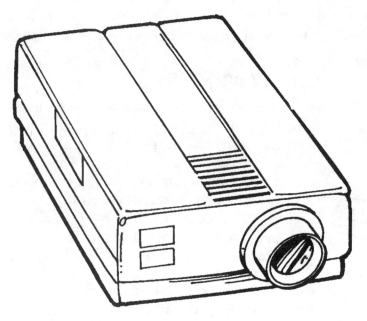

High-End Multimedia Projectors

These large-screen projectors are incredible and incredibly priced. It is not likely that you will see this all-in-one projector at your school unless you have found an extra $3,000 to $10,000 dollars in the student body account. These pieces of equipment are used to project computer, video, and laserdisc images onto a large movie screen. They are portable and usually include a sound system built in. Some examples include the LitePro 580 (InFocus), nFinity P115 (nView), and the Sharp XGE65OU (Sharp).

Advantages: durability, extremely clear picture even at large sizes

Disadvantages: $$$$

LCD Panels

Liquid crystal display, or LCD, panels work using the same technology as the digital watches many of us own. The difference is that the liquid crystals float between two sheets of glass that are embedded with electrodes. This panel is then placed on an overhead projector, connected to a computer or video source, and projected onto a large screen. These devices are still very pricey for use in a single classroom, with the average price ranging from just under $1,000 for a black-and-white model to several thousands for the top-of-the-line active matrix color model. In addition, most of these panels will require a special, extra-bright overhead projector, which is an additional cost. The most cost-effective use of an LCD panel is to share it among a

number of classes. The price of these devices has dropped dramatically in the past few years, and industry experts believe the cost will continue to decrease. Many suppliers will loan panels on a trial basis to schools which are interested in buying one.

OUTPUT DEVICES *(cont.)*

Advantages: large-screen projection

Disadvantages: $$$$ (Many models don't support the number of colors found in much of the newer CD-ROM software.)

PROJECTING ON THE TELEVISION

Older Computers?

A more affordable option for large-screen projection is the television. The Apple II, Laser, Radio Shack, and Commodore computers popular in the 1980s used regular video line signals. Because of this, these computers are very easy to display on a large-screen television. You simply split the video line coming out of the back of the computer by attaching a Y cable (available for under seven dollars at any Radio Shack store). This allows the computer to be seen at both its monitor and on the television. You can also videotape anything that is seen on the television. See the diagrams below for connecting.

If your television has a video line input, use this diagram.

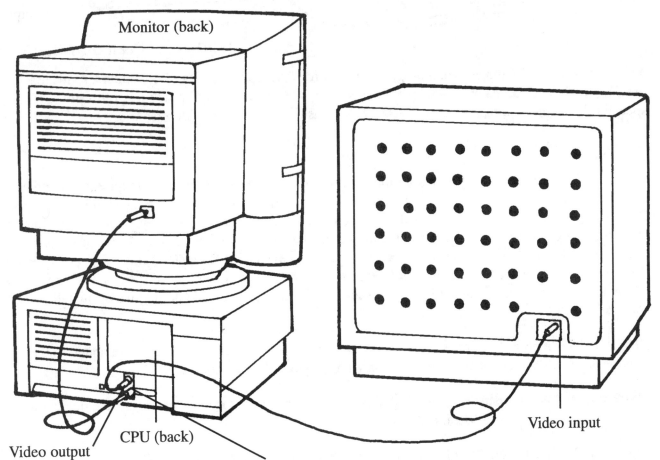

Monitor (back)

Video input

Video output

CPU (back)

Y Cord (1 male RCA connector to 2 females)

If your television does not have a video line input or you wish to videotape what is on the computer, use the diagram on page 18. If you do not have a VCR or a TV that has video line input or S video input, you will need to purchase an RF converter from a consumer electronics store like Radio Shack.

OUTPUT DEVICES *(cont.)*

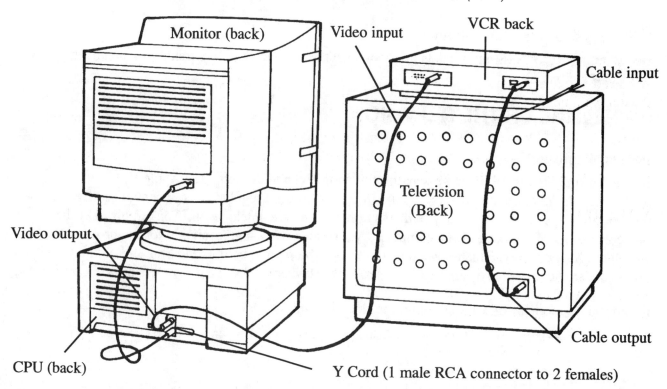

Tech Tip: Use VCR Companion, a program written for the Apple II series of computers, to make opening or closing credits on videotape projects. This inexpensive program will let you script several special effects, like rolling credits and dissolving transitions, for use in video reports.

Newer Computers

In order to accomplish the higher-resolution graphics we are used to on today's computers, computer companies such as IBM and Apple had to move away from line video used for television signals. Because of this, special hardware called video conversion or print-to-video boxes are needed to convert these high-resolution video signals to those which can be handled by televisions. These boxes are much more affordable than other large-screen projection devices. If televisions and VCRs are available, they give the user the added dimension of being able to videotape student presentations and projects for replay at school or home. Some of the video conversion devices available on the market include the following:

LTV Pro and Portable Pro (Focus Enhancements): Available as internal cards, they are added to the interior of the computer; as external boxes they are connected to the computer.

The Presenter Plus (Consumer Technology): Available as external connections only, these devices are available for both IBM and Macintosh.

TelevEyes (Digital Vision): Available in both external and internal options, this device is for IBM and Macintosh.

If your computer is an all-in-one design (CPU and monitor are built into the same case) and does not have an external video connector, you will need to purchase an adapter. These internally installed cards are usually around $75.00.

OUTPUT DEVICES *(cont.)*

Newer Computers *(cont.)*

If you do not have a VCR and your computer does not have a video line input or S video input, you will need an RF modulator available through Radio Shack and other consumer electronic stores. Use the diagram on page 18 as a reference only. Read the instructions that come with the unit carefully. Once you have the converter hooked up, tune the TV to the station that the VCR transmits on (usually channel 3 or 4), and switch the VCR to receive the Video In signal. This is usually accomplished by pushing the channel button on the VCR until AV or Video In is displayed. Sometimes there is a button on the VCR or its remote that switches the signal to Video In.

SPEAKERS

Most computers purchased in the last five years are equipped with, or have the capability of producing, sound. In order to produce sound, computers must have a sound card installed. You can usually find out if your computer has a sound card installed by looking for a speaker jack at the back panel of the computer. This is usually labeled with the word speaker or an icon that represents it. Computer speakers must be amplified in order to be heard. Make sure that amplified speakers are specified when purchasing.

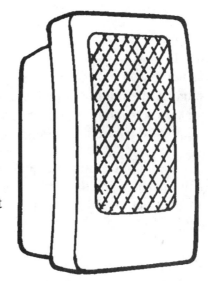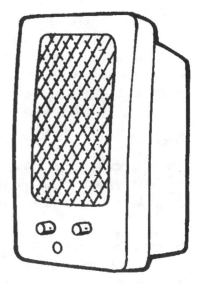

Amplified speakers require very little maintenance other than occasional cleaning. Make sure that volume levels during use stay below the level at which distortion is heard. If they do not, it can cause irreparable harm to the speaker mechanism.

CAPTURING PICTURES AND TEXT

One of the strengths of microcomputers is their ability to capture pictures and text so that they can be used in other applications. The following pieces of hardware are used to capture pictures and/or text.

SCANNERS

Scanners are peripheral devices that can take an image from the printed medium and digitize it for use in your computer. For instance, if your class is writing reports about ancient Greece and your textbook has an excellent picture of the Parthenon, you could use a scanner to save the image for use in reports. If the scanner has OCR (optical character recognition) software, scanned text can be used in a word processor and may be edited just as if you had typed it yourself.

OUTPUT DEVICES *(cont.)*

SCANNERS *(cont.)*

Scanners come in a variety of configurations, only two of which schools need or can afford: hand-held and flat-bed scanners. Hand-held scanners are less costly but provide a lower-quality image reproduction. These scanners are held in the hand and pulled across the document. Flat-bed scanners are more like photocopy machines. The document is placed on the scanner, and an image is taken. Flat-bed scanners are available in several different price ranges, depending much on the speed and resolution with which they scan a document. In most cases, schools require a color scanner that

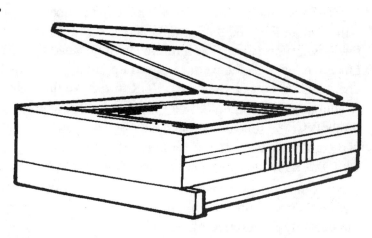

will accept up to a legal-size document at a minimum resolution of 1200 dpi (dots per inch). OCR software can be expensive if purchased separately; however, many scanners come with lesser capabilities. All scanners come with the software they require to function.

Maintenance for scanners usually consists of cleaning the glass or plastic scanning surface with a mild window cleaner. Avoid spraying the cleaner directly on the surface and use a soft cloth. Scratches in the glass will cause the transfer of lines onto scanned images.

DIGITAL CAMERAS

There are several digital cameras on the market that allow students and teachers to take pictures and input them directly from the devices into the computer. Since the cameras save the image in a digital format, they require no film. The pictures are stored as numbers in the memory of the camera. The memory can be transferred from the camera to the computer through a cable. The computer software can then assemble the digital information into an image that can be

used in a variety of writing and presentation programs. These cameras come in both black and white and color. Some models are portable, with the ability to be taken anywhere; however, others require the connection of a computer in order to be utilized.

These cameras take very little maintenance other than the cleaning of lenses with a soft cloth. Portable cameras require batteries; therefore, the batteries will have to be recharged or replaced occasionally.

OUTPUT DEVICES *(cont.)*

COMMUNICATION DEVICES

In order to communicate with other computers, for example, when using the Internet, a computer requires either a modem or network card. The use of a modem or network card depends on your connectivity (the way in which computers are connected).

NETWORK CARDS

If your school's computer is networked, your computer will require a network card similar to those used throughout the school. These devices allow your computer to share files, share devices (like printers), and communicate with one another. If your network is directly connected to the Internet, your network card will allow you to access information on other computers and networks around the world.

MODEMS

Most schools, however, do not have the resources for such costly connections to the Internet. In this case, modems are used to make this connection. These devices can be inside the computer in the form of a circuit board or external in the form of a box that is connected to the rear of the computer by a cable. The devices translate the digital information that your computer understands to analog or sound information that can be sent over a normal phone line. Because this translation takes time, modems are typically slower than directly connecting to a network. Modems are, however, much less expensive than the infrastructure required for a network and can offer the ability to fax documents from your computer. In order to access the Internet, one would only need a modem, dedicated phone line, and an Internet service provider (ISP). When shopping for a modem, one should look at the rate at which it can send and receive information. This is known as the baud rate and is expressed in bytes per second (bps).

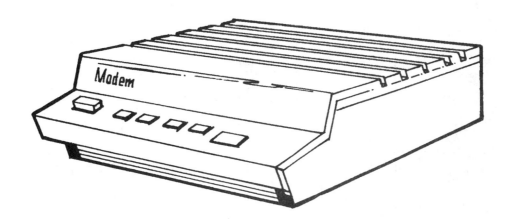

Modems take little or no maintenance. Keeping all electronic equipment clean prevents the buildup of heat, which can cause damage.

OUTPUT DEVICES *(cont.)*

Hardware Checkout Sheet

Type of Hardware	Equip. Number	Reserved From:	Reserved To:	Signature	Room Number	Additonal Information

COMPUTER SYSTEM WITH LABELS

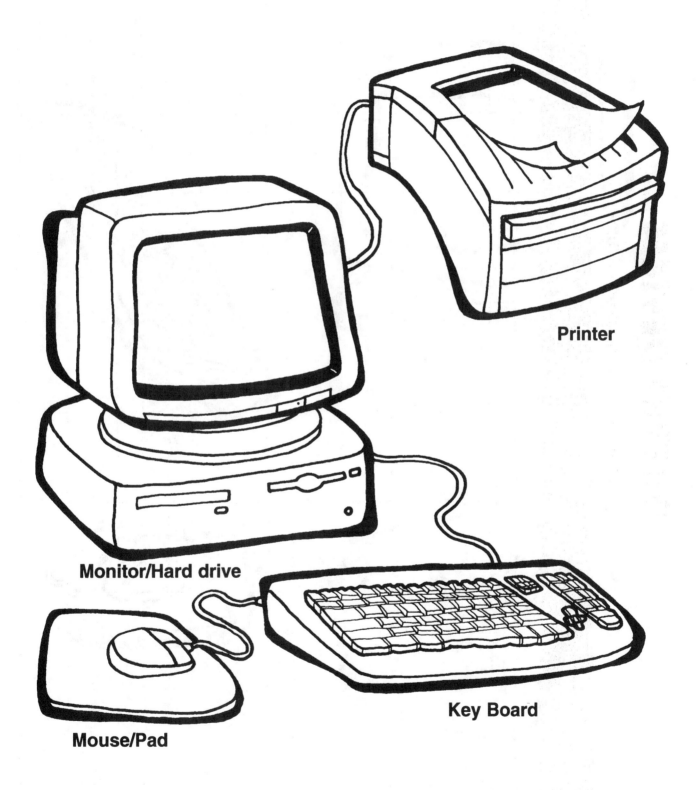

Printer

Monitor/Hard drive

Key Board

Mouse/Pad

COMPUTER SYSTEM WITHOUT LABELS

KEYBOARDING SKILLS

THIS PROJECT

With the prevalence of computers in both the classroom and home, there is a definite need for young students to become familiar with the keyboard. As students begin using computers more and more for writing their own stories, they may at times lose their flow of writing while searching for the correct keys. Familiarizing young students with the keyboard will help to eliminate the hunt-and-peck method and lead to a smoother writing activity. To address this need, you will find a graphic of a Macintosh keyboard as well as an IBM keyboard on pages 26 and 27, along with some classroom suggestions for keyboarding activities.

BEFORE BEGINNING

- Using a keyboard, demonstrate to your students the correct finger positions on the home row and how those fingers remain on the home row even when reaching for letters above or below the home row. Have your students color in the home row of keys so they stand out.
- Show your students how the thumb is used to press the space bar.
- Duplicate, enlarge to approximately 150 percent, and laminate the keyboard blackline masters found on pages 26 and 27 for each student and then give them the responsibility of taking care of their keyboards.

Keyboarding Activities

Using one of the keyboards on pages 26 and 27, the following activities can be used as transition-time activities in your classroom—those three minutes before recess and after math, before going to lunch, or even before the end of the day.

- Make a list of the week's spelling words on either the board or an overhead. Then have your students practice typing each word.
- Have your students practice locating special keys on the keyboard (e.g., tab, space bar, return, shift, delete, etc.).
- Write a math problem on the board and have your students type in the numbers to match the problem.
- Have your students practice writing their friends' names, using the shift key for capital letters.

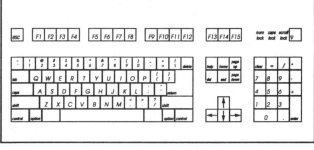

- Write a letter on the board and have your students find that letter on their keyboards.
- You might want to choose a special word of the day and have your students practice typing it.
- Have students practice typing holiday names. The capital letters are good practice for using the shift key.

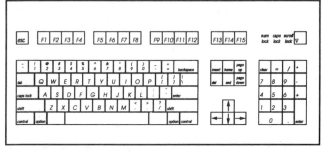

- Write the day and date on the board and have your students type it on their keyboards.

KEYBOARDING SKILLS *(cont.)*

MAC KEYBOARD

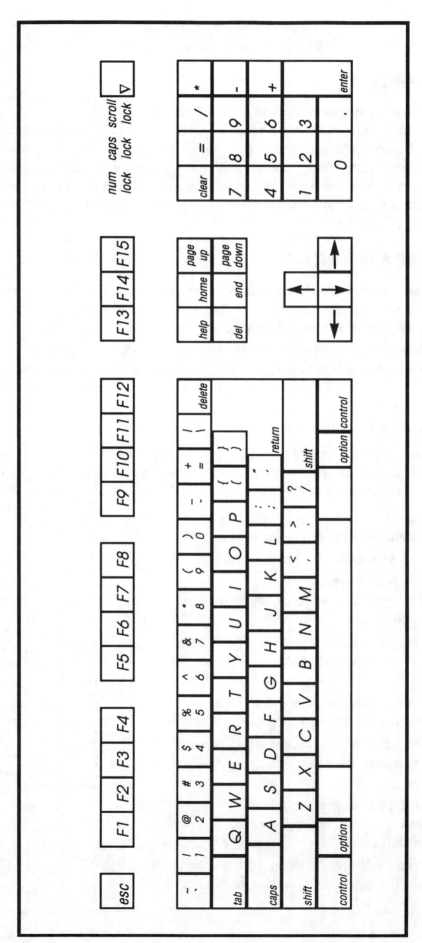

KEYBOARDING SKILLS *(cont.)*

IBM KEYBOARD

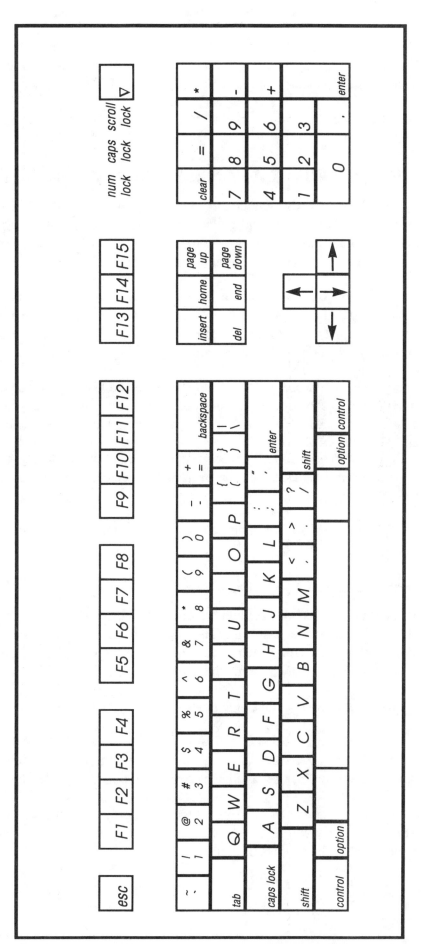

THE ONE-COMPUTER CLASSROOM

Having one computer in the classroom can be a blessing in disguise. Although you hear, "When is it my turn?" over and over, especially when you are in the middle of a fabulous presentation on regrouping, you can solve many of the inherent problems by good management techniques.

You will be introduced to several workable procedures in this section so that you and the computer remain friends.

USING THE COMPUTER AS AN ELECTRONIC CHALKBOARD

Fortunately for educators and students, the computer programs produced today have graphics that are far superior to that which we can find quickly in the library or that we can produce ourselves without a lengthy time and talent involvement. An example of this is the video clips included on *The Animals 2.0* CD-ROM which show animals in action in vividly filmed sequences.

There is really no reason that you cannot have a small group gather around your regular-sized computer monitor for a guided lesson. The software available today lends itself to adding depth to your lessons. Technology itself is just a tool to help you deliver the curriculum, whether by aiding in the presentation of a lesson, helping with productivity, or helping with the dreaded teacher job of recordkeeping.

Hook your computer to the TV and illustrate your directed lesson or place an LCD panel on the overhead projector and show the class some software as an enhancement to your lessons. Using a projection device, students can show their completed creative work to the class.

Your school might purchase an LCD panel which you can borrow to use in your classroom. You simply attach it to your computer, place it on the overhead projector, turn it all on, and your presentation proceeds.

With a careful selection of software, you can use large-screen presentations to greatly enhance the delivery of curriculum content.

AN EXAMPLE OF A LARGE-SCREEN WHOLE-CLASS LESSON

Your kindergarten class has been studying geometric shapes. You have had them point out all the different shapes found in the classroom. They have looked at many excellent books about shapes. Your class has done art projects using squares, rectangles, circles, and triangles, and now they are ready to culminate their study and show how much they have learned.

Let's use technology to review the shape names and the differences between the shapes.

A good computer program to use for this culminating activity is *Kid Pix* or *Kid Pix Studio*. Using either of these programs, you can make a slide show without much time and effort. Refer to pages 111–119 for directions on making a "Shapes Are All Around Us Slide Show."

You can even show your slide show using a big-screen projection device, and your class will be in awe of the presentation. They will be able to correctly identify all the shapes you used in your presentation and will want to make slide shows of their own.

THE ONE-COMPUTER CLASSROOM *(cont.)*

STUDENT MANAGEMENT

Because of limited individual student computer time, most of the production work has to be done before arriving at the computer. The school versions of most educational software products include excellent lesson plans for using the program on the computer and for offline activities. If it is a productivity program, there are usually printouts of the graphics that your students can choose to use.

A suggestion that works well in any computer configuration, is to duplicate the pages of graphic printouts, mount them on file folders, and laminate them. This will give a longer life to the graphic printouts in your classroom.

Students can use these laminated printouts as reference material when creating their own projects. They can use storyboards to plan their graphics and text. Refer to pages 174 and 175 for blackline masters of storyboards. When they arrive at a computer, their time can be used productively because of all the preplanning they have already done.

THE ONE-COMPUTER CLASSROOM *(cont.)*

STUDENT MANAGEMENT *(cont.)*

Small-Group Activity

Many primary classrooms use centers and small-group activities in their classroom management. If you use small groups for directed teaching, you can use the computer as part of your lesson. The computer makes an ideal part of a learning center surrounded by books and other reference material relating to the subject of the center. For example, a science center based on a wild animal theme might include reference books, activity sheets, and a computer program that students use for their research. After ample time is given to research, a productivity program can be placed in the center for students to use to create habitats for wild animals. The bulletin board above the center can be used to display the students' work.

Place a list of students under a piece of plastic taped to the desk so that students can place checks next to their names after they have used the computer station. You might want to refer to the list daily in case you need to start students there first if they haven't been able to secure turns on their own.

If you are using three-group rotation for your classroom management in reading or math, you might want to include the computer as part of the rotation. While one group is with you, the second group is doing their activity sheets, and the third group is working either on the computer itself or drafting their material to be inputted into the computer when time allows. Use your normal rotation times and watch the computer become an integral part of the three-group rotation. It is essential in this situation that students have their own disks on which to save material. The disks are very inexpensive now, especially if your school buys them in bulk. The disks travel on with students to the next grade and can prove to be excellent electronic portfolios. Even if you are not doing the three-group rotation, it is equally essential for students to have their own disks. The pride that they exhibit in having disks with their own names on them is visible through their care of the disks.

THE ONE-COMPUTER CLASSROOM (cont.)

COOPERATIVE LEARNING GROUPS

A one-computer classroom can make good use of the technology by using it for a focal point in a cooperative learning strategy. You assign to your class a particular subject which they are to use to produce a project that can be shown to the class.

When the group meets, each student is given a role in the production of the project. One student is the scribe and takes notes on the group discussions as to how they want to proceed with the project. One student heads the research team as to what will be included in the project. One student is assigned to input the art work and the other to input the text. The students work with an individual storyboard, or the group works with a large storyboard that can be seen by all.

SCHEDULING TIME ON THE COMPUTER

If you are using the computer in a situation where it stands alone and is to be used by as many students as possible during the week, you will need to decide on a schedule for use. Depending upon your preference, you might want to schedule blocks of time where the students are assigned to the computer in pairs or small groups, or you might prefer the computers being in use all day with students working in pairs for a shorter length of time. In either case you will need to draw up a schedule and post it in plain sight. Young students will watch the time carefully, waiting for their turn.

SCHEDULING EXAMPLE

When assigning students to a block of time, you can group them in mixed ability groups, and they can choose a name or you can color-code them (blue group, yellow group, etc.). For example, if the purple group is on the computer during the math block, the four to five students in the group may work on the computer during that time. During each week or each unit, every group should have computer time during every block. For some units, the technology component may be a group activity so all students in the group are contributing. When you assign an individual activity, students take turns at the computer based on who is prepared and ready for the technology activity. This method may sound like a scheduling nightmare, but you would be surprised at how easily students are able to adjust once a routine is set.

MIXED ABILITY GROUPS				
Blue Group	Yellow Group	Red Group	Purple Group	Green Group
BOB	AUSTIN	DARYL	RENEE	JOHN
DAWN	GEORGE	DIANE	KIMBERLY	JILL
KYLE	MIKE	BILL	JASON	ERIN
BARBARA	BYRON	PAMELA	GARY	DOREEN
MANUEL	JOE	CAROL	JUAN	TERESA

THE ONE-COMPUTER CLASSROOM *(cont.)*

SCHEDULING EXAMPLE *(cont.)*

To keep track of whose group is scheduled for computer time during the day, use a paper clip to hang a string from the ceiling over the computer. At each block changeover, hang the coordinating color of construction paper over the technology center. This signals the group that at some point during the small-group activities, they may work on the computer.

Sample Schedule:

Block	Monday	Tuesday	Wednesday	Thursday	Friday
Math	Purple	Blue	Red	Yellow	Green
Writer's Workshop	Blue	Red	Yellow	Green	Purple
Thematic Unit	Green	Yellow	Blue	Purple	Red
Language Arts	Yellow	Green	Purple	Red	Blue

Everyone Gets Computer Time

Making sure all your students have the opportunity to work on the computer can be very difficult. There are ways to make it easier to manage for you and your students. Choose a visual way to display who has and has not been to the computer. Regardless of how you schedule student time on the computer, this is a successful way to make sure one person is not monopolizing the computer. The following methods allow you, the teacher, and the students to do a quick scan to see who has had a recent turn on the computer and who still needs the opportunity.

Craft Sticks

Materials: marker, craft stick for every student, two jars/cups

Put each student's name on a craft stick. Label one jar "not yet" and one jar "been there." At the beginning of the week or unit, all students start out in the "not yet" jar. Once they have had their turns on the computer, they must put their craft sticks in the "been there" jar. This does not mean they cannot use a computer a second time. Whenever the computer is available, it is fair game. However, it does mean that students in the "not yet" jar can bump a student off the computer by taking their craft sticks from the "not yet" jar. You never want your computer to gather dust when it can be productive; however, you do need to allow opportunity for all students.

Clothespins

Materials: poster board (one piece), one clothespin for each student

Put each student's name on a clothespin. Draw a line down the middle of the poster board. The left side is reserved for students who have not been to the computer; the right side is for those who have been. Once they have had a turn on the computer, they move their clothespins to the other side. Perhaps on this side you could list alternative independent activities once each student has worked on a computer (writer's workshop, reading corner, research, puzzle center, etc.).

THE ONE-COMPUTER CLASSROOM (cont.)

RULES

Have specific behavior expectations for students in the computer lab. Because the computer lab is different from the classroom, you may want to set specific guidelines for student behavior. As you introduce these rules, show the students exactly what it looks like if a student is following a rule and discuss examples of what might constitute breaking a rule. Use a role-playing exercise, if necessary, to demonstrate acceptable behavior.

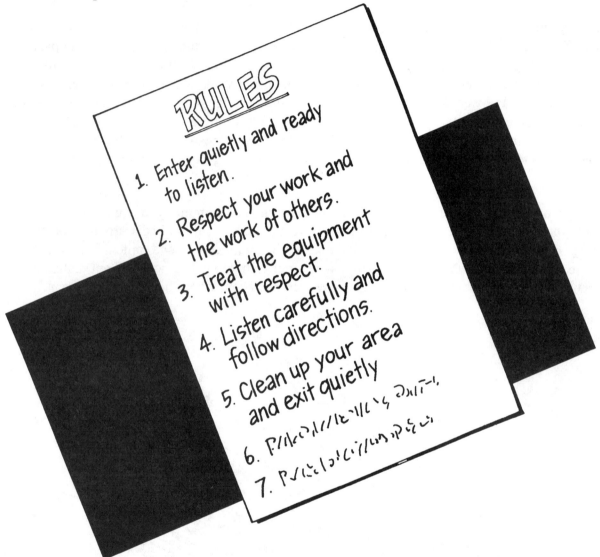

Set up very clear consequences for breaking the rules and be consistent.

Sample Consequences

First offense: warning

Second offense: five minutes off the computer

Third offense: note home to parents and lose remaining computer time

THE ONE-COMPUTER CLASSROOM (cont.)

WHERE SHOULD I PUT IT?

Primary classrooms are usually crowded, busy places with lots of movement by both the teacher, other adults, and students. This fact is of prime concern when deciding on computer placement in the classroom. Before setting up your classroom for this technological addition, it is important to ask yourself this question—What will I primarily use the computer for? The answer to that question will greatly determine the "home base" where your computer will be located most of the time.

If you will mostly be using the classroom computer as a presentation and cooperative learning tool for your lessons, then you will want to set up your classroom similar to the diagram found on page 35. This type of setup will also be beneficial for student presentations. If the fundamental use for the classroom computer is more of a work station for independent work, research, or long-term group projects, then you will want to set up your classroom similar to the diagram found on page 36. Let an extra table remain near the computer station so cooperative learning groups will have a place to meet. Or, if your computer-using plans mostly entail recordkeeping, correspondence, electronic portfolio management, and overall personal assistance to help manage your day, look at the diagram found on page 37.

While each of the diagrams are set up with the primary function in mind, you can see the paths for easy flow into the other computer uses as well. Most educators in one-computer classrooms find the computer is used for a variety of purposes and ends up being moved around quite a bit. How fortunate we are to teach at a time when we can control where our technology tool will be kept, unlike our nineteenth-century predecessors who did not have a choice about where the blackboard went.

THE ONE-COMPUTER CLASSROOM *(cont.)*
DIAGRAM 1

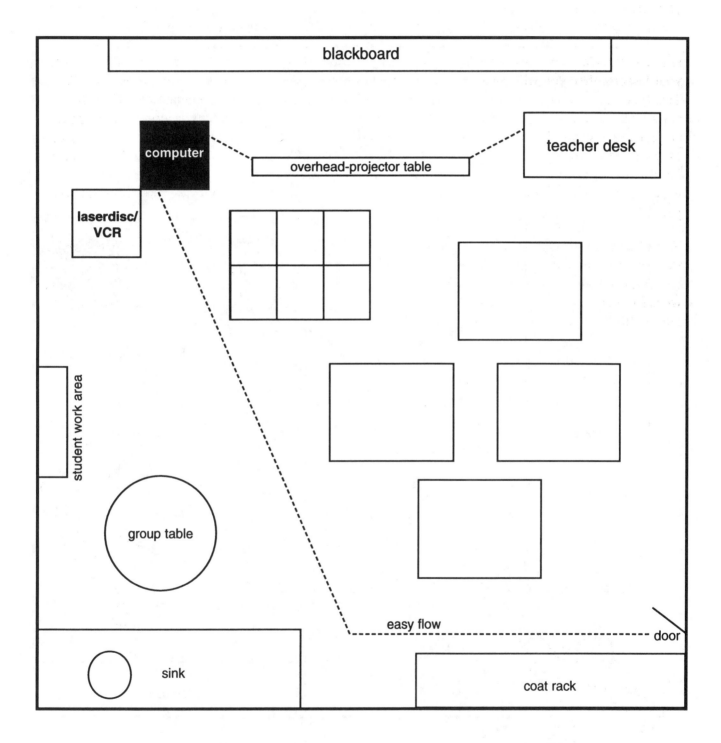

THE ONE-COMPUTER CLASSROOM *(cont.)*

DIAGRAM 2

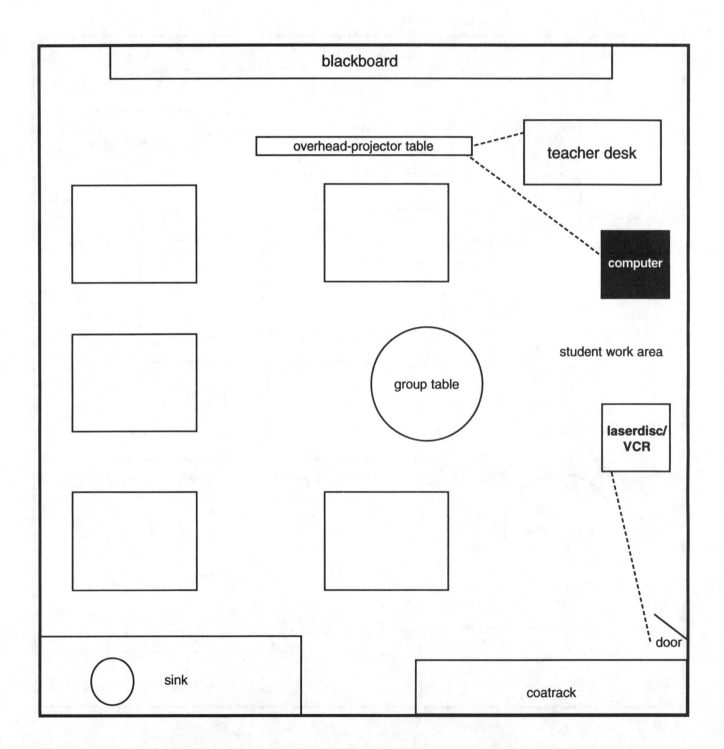

THE ONE-COMPUTER CLASSROOM (cont.)

DIAGRAM 3

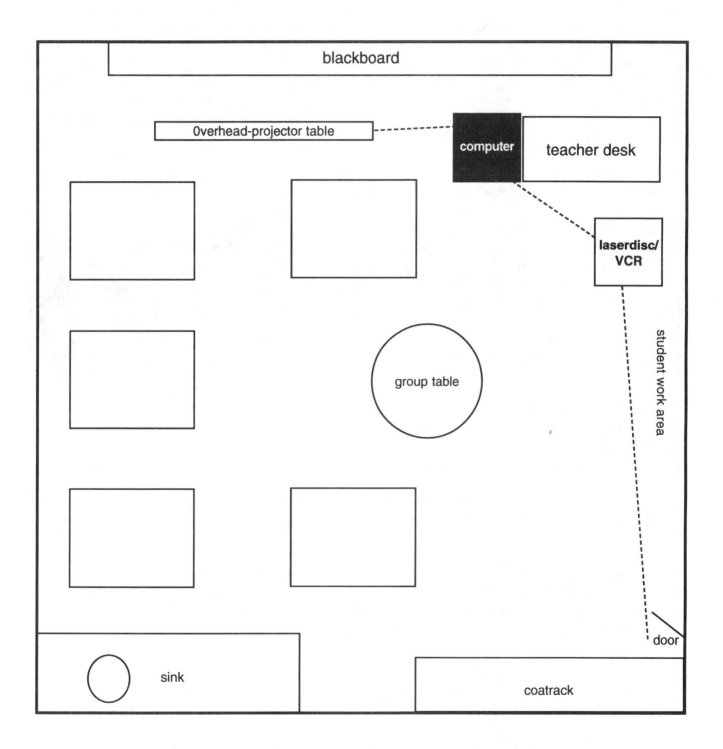

THE ONE-COMPUTER CLASSROOM (cont.)

WHAT SHOULD I HAVE ALONG WITH THE COMPUTER?

It is recommended that students have their own disks with their names on them as soon as they know how to save their work. Place these disks in a plastic disk container next to the computer for ready access. Many of the disks today come preformatted and ready for use. When you place them in the computer, all the computer wants to know is the name of the disk. Type in students' names and the year for their disks. This way, when they put them in the computer to save their work, they see their names on the screen and know it is OK to save. At the end of the semester or year, the disks can travel on with students to the next class. In schools that have a high rate of transiency, the disks act as reminders to the students of their time with you, if you give their disks to them when they leave. You can recycle used disks by inserting them in your computer and requesting "erase disk" from the main menu. This erases the disk so that it is ready for a new student. Macintoshes can take IBM formatted disks and ready them for use with the Mac.

Equip your computer with an attachment that has a large clip to hold work the students are inputting. Usually this attachment has *Velcro®* to hold it to your computer monitor. This is also handy for your use. One commercial name is Computer Hands, and the cost is normally below five dollars. This product, or one similar to it, can be found in many educational software catalogs. Refer to page 131 for a list of some catalogue companies.

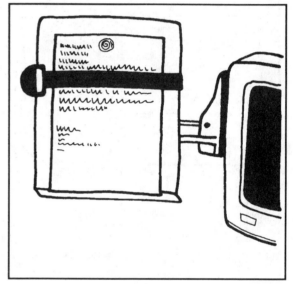

Hopefully, you have a printer and there is room to place it next to the computer. Students will love to see their work come out of a printer.

One publication from Teacher Created Materials has task cards ready for you to copy, mount, laminate, and place next to the computer. *Kid Pix for Terrified Teachers* contains over 28 cross-curricular projects for your students.

Use your bulletin board to display your students' publications, as well as place their published books in the library. *Kid Pix for Terrified Teachers* has a myriad of suggestions for bulletin board displays using its projects.

Computer Tip: Place a red cup and a blue cup next to the computer monitor. The red cup should be placed on top of the monitor when help is needed. The blue cup should be placed on top of the monitor when something cool has been done on the computer. Both of these methods will prevent students from constantly disturbing your class.

THE MULTICOMPUTER CLASSROOM

What strings did you pull to rate more than one computer in your classroom? Whatever it took, you are lucky! Now you can have much more productivity and interactive involvement in your primary classroom. More small-group activities and cooperative groups can be engaged at the same time.

Those of you with more than one primary language spoken in the classroom can seize this as an extra opportunity for English acquisition. As children work in small groups at the computer, English becomes the common language as students try to solve problems and design projects.

Many of the computer programs for primary children use graphics to explain content, and the English language learner can take advantage of this to help with concept development. There are also available for the primary child many programs that have auditory help that ranges all the way from reading stories to problem explanations to verbal directions. All these auditory programs help the English-learning students, along with the Englishspeaking children, use their auditory mode for learning.

In this age of technology, students can use all their modes of learning while working on the computer; the interactive use of the keyboard provides tactile response, the sounds of the programs entice the auditory learner, and the visual displays help the visual learner.

There are two diagrams to use as suggestions for location of your computer lab. The diagram found on page 40 is similar to the one on page 35. This strategy is beneficial in that it allows for easy passage of a mobile computer which is to be connected with an overhead projector, to be used for class presentations, to be used as a teacher's assistant, or to be hooked up to the laserdisc player. With the computer pod located in the front of the room, however, there is the potential challenge of keeping noncomputer-using students focused on the task or lesson at hand. If this is a concern, try setting your classroom up according to the diagram found on page 41, with the computer pod away from the front of the room.

THE MULTICOMPUTER CLASSROOM *(cont.)*

DIAGRAM 1

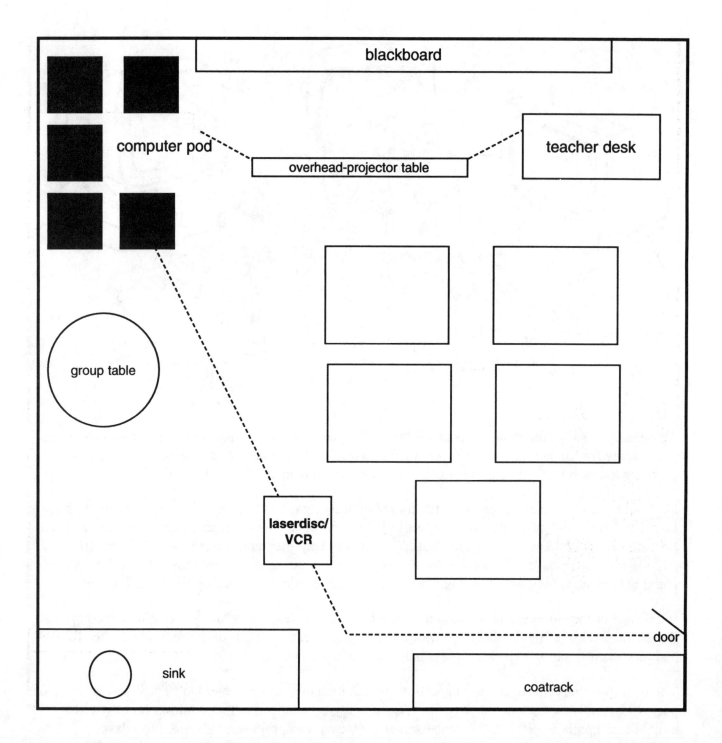

THE MULTICOMPUTER CLASSROOM *(cont.)*
DIAGRAM 2

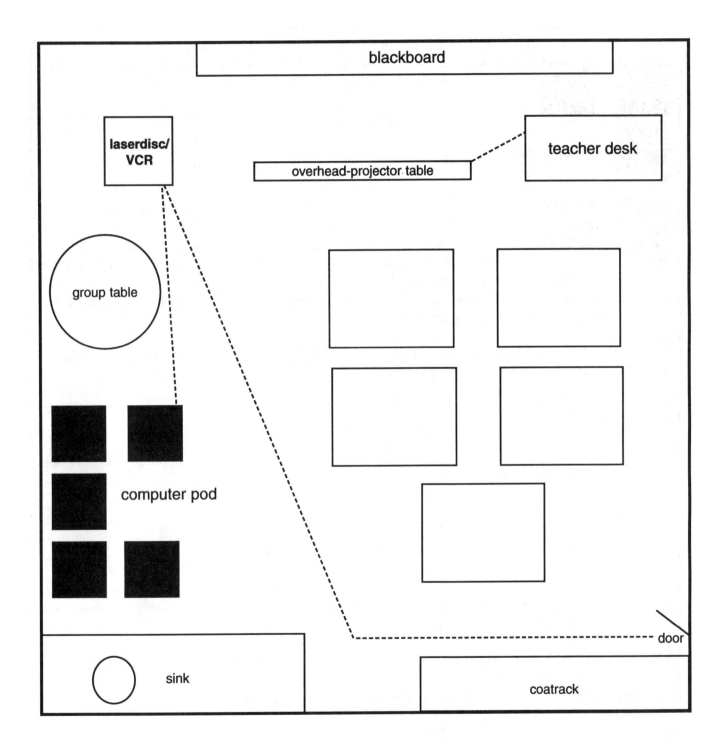

THE COMPUTER LAB

Many schools today arrange their computers in a room that is dedicated to technology which they then designate as a computer lab or tech center. Not only are there computers in the lab, but often the lab becomes a media center for the use of students and teachers alike.

In many cases teachers bring their classes into the computer lab based on a specific schedule. The computer lab is most often supervised by a technology aide. In some schools money has been allocated to hire a teacher to be in charge of the lab while in other schools volunteers have been trained to take charge of the lab. Some facilities prefer the lab arrangement because each student is assured of a specific amount of time using the computer. In the lab students work on various types of programs ranging from drill and practice to multimedia production.

THE BASIC COMPUTER LAB

Take a look at a primary class as they use the computer lab. The students have written stories in their classrooms about their favorite animals. They have edited their work in the classroom and are now entering the computer lab, holding the edited copies of their stories. As they enter the lab, they select their own disks, which have all of their work saved on them, from a classroom disk box container. Each student goes to an assigned computer and sits quietly, waiting for directions to be given by the lab tech. When the class is ready, using the large TV at the front of the room, the tech shows them how to open *Storybook Weaver* on their computers. For this day's lesson the tech knows that if students can just input their text, they will have accomplished enough.

The tech will show them how to choose a graphic at the next lab session. It probably will take three sessions to complete their text, graphic placement, and publishing.

The students carefully input their writing. Suddenly there are two red cups on top of computers. The teacher goes over to one of the computers and helps the student with a problem.

A blue cup appears on top of a computer which is being used by a student who is jumping up and down on his/her seat. The lab tech walks over to the student and admires his/her work. It seems that he/she has written his/her text using one font for the title and another font for the remainder of the page and is very excited about this achievement.

They don't have enough time today to finish inputting their text, so when the lab tech says that they have five more minutes of time left in the lab, students then insert their own disks into the drive and save their work to it. The lab tech reminds the students how to save to disk. Of course, this has been shown to the students previously many times. The students take their disks, and as they are dismissed they replace them in the classroom disk box.

The next time in the lab, the students will continue inputting their stories about their favorite animals. The lab tech will also review with the students, using the projection device, how to place graphics in their stories, and they will finish the text and begin to place the graphics.

HOW DID THIS ALL COME ABOUT?

It took a lot of planning on the part of the school and community for the school to get to the point of having a working computer lab. First, a technology planning committee composed of staff and community was formed, and technology goals for the school were devised.

THE COMPUTER LAB *(cont.)*

HOW DID THIS ALL COME ABOUT? *(cont.)*

In the beginning, the school had several computers and printers dispersed among the classrooms. The teachers suggested at faculty meetings that they really felt that the computers would be used more and aligned more with the school's technology goal if they were placed in one specific site. Several teachers said that they did not feel comfortable teaching students about technology and using technology themselves. After much discussion, a vote was taken of the staff and community, and the school was on its way to a computer lab. Now the real work began.

SETTING UP THE HARDWARE

An empty classroom was available, so that became the site of the lab-to-be. The district agreed to provide the muscle power to move the computers into the empty room, and they also agreed to provide the expertise for the electrical placements. The computers were set up on tables that seated two per table around the perimeter of the room so that the center of the room remained free for movement and class demonstrations. The lab tech could have all the children sit in the middle and watch the demonstration on the large TV monitor.

The printers were placed at the end of each set of three tables. The teachers thought that having the printers near the computers provided extra incentive for word processing and graphic design.

One of the important points raised by the teachers about having a lab was that they wanted a station in the lab where they could work on their own materials.

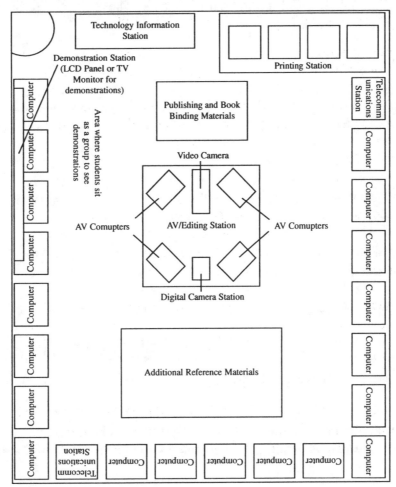

CHOOSING THE SOFTWARE

Before choosing software for the computer lab, the goals of the technology plan and the computer lab in general had to be addressed. The main technology goal in this particular school was to use it for increasing the productivity of students in the area of language arts.

The technology committee also stated that the curriculum of the district must be taken into account when choosing software.

The subgoals included using multimedia for teacher presentations and using the computers as a tool to assist teachers in recordkeeping. A less prominent goal was to use technology for computer-aided instruction.

Four computers were placed in the library for student and librarian use. Purchases of reference CD-ROMs were made. A book-tracking software package was also purchased for library use.

Now, the task at hand was choosing specific software programs for the lab.

For aid in choosing software for your school please, refer to pages 128–131 in this book for guidance. There is a checklist that can be used in assessing software. There are also many software descriptions on pages 132–166 that should help you in choosing software to preview.

This school chose several programs at each level: primary, middle, and upper. They chose a few programs that they felt could be used throughout the grades. These seemed to be the ones most used in the lab and throughout the school.

TRAINING THE STAFF

Several sources were used to train the staff—personnel provided by the district and school level personnel who were knowledgeable in technology. The tech committee surveyed the staff and found that quite a few of the teachers had technology training before they began teaching, and some teachers had taken college courses just because they found technology fascinating.

In several sessions the staff had been shown how to use the pieces of software that would be used across the grade levels. These sessions focused on having the staff produce or publish a product. (You can use the lessons in this book to in-service teachers.)

Each member of the tech committee and several other teachers have agreed to learn one piece of software in depth and then help other teachers with the use of that program.

ACHIEVING THE PRIMARY GOALS

The lab opened and the students, staff, and community were very excited about the progress. On Back to School night there were more parents in the computer lab than in the classrooms at any one time. Grandparents could be seen smiling and chatting proudly while viewing the work of their grandchildren.

The school staff realizes that this is only the beginning of their school's movement into using technology as a tool. Through constant involvement of teachers and community, the school will continue with its forward movement.

USING ASSESSMENT WITH PRIMARY STUDENTS

Since by common understanding, authentic assessment is based upon assessing students in a way that meets their individual learning styles, using technology for authentic assessment is a natural. If we are to use Howard Gardner's theory of multiple intelligences as a way to consider different learning abilities, then using technology as a basic tool follows easily. Gardner has currently identified seven intelligences:

The Seven Intelligences

1. **Linguistic**—engaged by working with words in games and through writing

2. **Logical-mathematical**—engaged by numbers, computers, and reasoning games

3. **Spatial**—engaged by artistic activities, reading maps and charts, solving jigsaw puzzles, and seeing patterns

4. **Musical**—engaged by listening to music, playing instruments, and being aware of nonverbal sounds and patterns in speech and music

5. **Bodily-kinesthetic**—engaged by movement, sports activities, and using body language for communication

6. **Interpersonal**—interested in working and learning in collaboration with other people

7. **Intrapersonal**—interested in working and learning alone

---

USING ASSESSMENT WITH PRIMARY STUDENTS *(cont.)*

Upon reviewing the seven levels of multiple intelligences, it is amazing how many of these intelligences are encompassed in using productivity software. The impact of using productivity software is most felt by the student who doesn't shine on the paper and pencil tests. Students can express their intelligence through creation and presentation, whereas normally the assessments are very restrictive.

If we are to use Bloom's Levels of Cognition as our guide to assessment, *Kid Pix* again provides an avenue of assessment for the total child. For a refresher on Bloom's Taxonomy, listed are the six levels of cognition from simplest to most complex: evaluation, synthesis, analysis, application, comprehension, and knowledge You might want to have students use the self-assessment tool on page 47 as attachments to their publications so that you can get a feeling for their personal assessments. Some of the projects have specific evaluation forms.

From Multiple Intelligences: The Theory into Practice. Howard Gardner. New York: Basic Books, 1993.

USING ASSESSMENT WITH PRIMARY STUDENTS *(cont.)*

PROJECT ASSESSMENT FORM

Name _____

Date _____

This is how I felt about the project_____

_____

_____

_____

	Yes	No
I followed directions.	_____	_____
I used the computer well.	_____	_____
I planned ahead.	_____	_____
I can help others with this project.	_____	_____

INTERNET IN THE PRIMARY CLASSROOM

Internet, e-mail, World Wide Web, search engines! You may ask how does these fit into the primary curriculum in the classroom.

There is a definite place in your teacher resources for the Internet and all the connectivity that it brings. Young students, too, can benefit from the interactive tours of sites around the world. They can also exchange their writings and illustrations with children all over the world. Best of all, the Internet connects you with teachers all over the world who are teaching units and concepts similar to the ones you are teaching.

The following is a short and simplified explanation of the World Wide Web for your background information. All you need to connect to the Web is a computer, modem, telephone and a service provider who gives you the software to connect to the Net. Many school districts throughout the world are providing access to the Internet for their students and teachers. Research how you can get on the Net, and off you'll go on an interesting journey provided by technology.

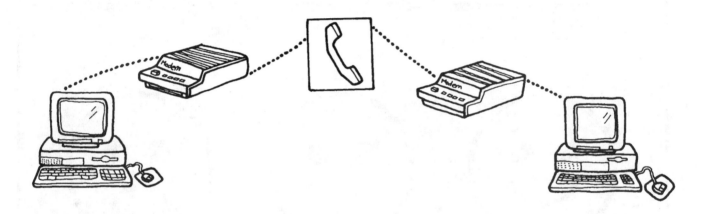

WHAT IS THE INTERNET?

The Internet is comprised of millions of computers all over the world which are all hooked together. These computers communicate through satellite, buried fiberoptic cable, telephone lines, and other data links. All of these computers can connect regardless of their hardware brand. Your Macintosh can talk with a Windows machine in England without a problem.

WHAT IS ON THE INTERNET?

Newsgroups: Newsgroups are discussion groups on all kinds of topics. The messages are posted to the group and anyone can answer.

World Wide Web: The Web is comprised of millions of documents stored on computers all over the world.

E-Mail: Send and receive electronic messages around the world in minutes. All you need is an e-mail address for yourself and the person to whom you are sending mail. E-mail is also used for sending documents around the world.

INTERNET IN THE PRIMARY CLASSROOM *(cont.)*

WHAT IS ON THE INTERNET? *(cont.)*

Web Browsers: The Web browser is used for finding information through a search that you instigate simply by typing in key words for it to use as a guide. For example, you need to find more information on grant availability for educational technology. Go to one of the search engines and type in the words "education grants technology," and then click on the search button. Off the search engine goes to explore the Web for items related to what you are looking for. It presents you with a list of related items. Look through the list and click on any that interest you for your search. You will now be taken to a Web page that gives you information or points you to another place on the Web for your information. Amazing!

There are many search engines on the Web, each one having a slightly different look from the other. Explore to see which ones you prefer. Here are a few of the most prominent search engines as of today: Magellan, Infoseek, Alta Vista, Yahoo!, Excite, Lycos, Infoseek, Netscape, and Mosaic.

Listed below are some sites that are especially helpful for teachers. Type in their addresses (URL) when you reach the World Wide Web main page, and you will be taken to the sites.

HOW DO I USE IT?

Teacher Uses: Need some new ideas for lesson plans? Log on to your computer's Internet server and type in . . . http://www.sdserv.org/tie/lessons.html for lesson plans for all content areas.

Try education.indiana.edu/cas/adol/adol.html for more lesson plans on the Internet.

More lessons and activities are found at www.kn.pacbell.com/wired/bluewebn/index.html.

Scott Foresman has a Web site at aw.com/sf/teaindex.htm where you can find lesson plans and links to other sites.

The Thematic Unit Archives, collaborative lessons for pre-K to 12, are found at faldo.atmos.uiuc.edu/TUA-Home.html

If you type in an address and on the screen appears the dreaded "404: URL not found" this is generally caused by a typing error in the address you typed in. The link location may have changed slightly since being published. Try typing in just the first few commands and see if that makes a difference.

To reach a search engine if it is not listed on the menu page of your server, type in the following:
Yahoo!: http://www.yahoo.com
WebCrawler: http://webcrawler.com
Lycos: http://www.lycos.com
InfoSeek: http://www2.Infoseek.com
Excite: http://www.excite.com
AltaVista: http://www.altavista.digital.com

Use search engines to research materials that you need for your teaching. Check facts on everything from fishing sites to the structure of the Chinese government easily on the Net.

INTERNET IN THE PRIMARY CLASSROOM *(cont.)*

CLASSROOM USE IN THE PRIMARY GRADES

Hook up your computer to a large-screen monitor and take a guided tour of the White House at http://www.whitehouse.gov/. You can even hear Socks, the First Cat, meow!

Connect with Discovery Channel School at http://school.discovery.com to enter the documentary libraries of Discovery Channel and The Learning Channel. This site also includes lesson plans, activities, and links to related sites.

Visit a beginner's guide to astronomy written for smaller children and presented in an easy-to-read text at http://guinan.gsfc.nasa.gov/K12/StarChild.html.

View the collection of the Metropolitan Museum of Art at http://www.metmuseum.org.

There are many books available listing web sites for you to use in the classroom for students and yourself.

Internet-based Books Published by Teacher Created Materials:

Gardner, Paul. *Internet for Teachers and Parents.* Teacher Created Materials, 1996.

Haag, Tim. *Internet for Kids.* Teacher Created Materials, 1996.

Haag, Tim. *Internet for Kids* (Intermediate). Teacher Created Materials, 1996.

Spaulding, Sandy. *Internet for Kids* (Challenging). Teacher Created Materials, 1997.

Internet-based Books Published by Other Companies:

Butler, Mark. *How to Use the Internet.* Ziff-Davis Press, 1994.

Ellsworth, Jill H. *Education on the Internet.* Sams Publishing, 1994.

Hoffman, Paul E. *Netscape and the World Wide Web for Dummies.* IDG Books Worldwide, Inc., 1995.

Johnson, Keith. *Using Gopher.* Que Corporation, 1995.

Krol, Ed. *The Whole Internet User's Guide & Catalog.* O'Reilly & Associates, Inc., 1992.

Levine, John R. and Carol Baroudi. *The Internet for Dummies.* IDG Books Worldwide, Inc., 1994.

FINDING MONEY FOR TECHNOLOGY GRANT WRITING

As we are well aware, there is only so much money available for education, and where that money is spent has to be carefully chosen. One way that the primary classroom teacher can augment the technology available for the classroom is with funding through grants that support technology.

LOOKING FOR GRANT SOURCES

The best place to begin the search for a grant source is within your school district. Make the district aware that you are willing to write a grant for technology monies. Many districts have their own district grant programs to encourage developing model projects and programs for sharing them. Your state might also be a funding source. If your state has educational technology organizations, that is a good place to start on your search for a funding source.

Corporations are also a source of grant monies. Search out large organizations in your community to see if they are funding school-based grant programs.

The Internet has become a great resource for finding grant sources. Begin your search in the educational area of the various search engines. Search using various key words until you have narrowed your search to a manageable number. You will find national, state, local, and foundation grant sources on the Web.

GETTING READY TO WRITE

You researched through your grants office at the district level, have read pertinent books and educational articles, actually surfed the Net, and are now ready to "get it down in writing."

You have the grant application in hand and are ready to begin the writing process. You have noted the directions for the grant application and see that each section must be only one typed page in ten-point type and double-spaced. It must be signed by the principal and two parents along with the grant writers. It is due on a specific date at the county office. You know that the above directions must be followed to the letter or the grant will be eliminated before even being evaluated.

OK. IT IS NOW TIME TO BEGIN!

Organization, planning, and insight into what the application reviewers are looking for are your keys to a successful grant. Enlist the aid of several colleagues to write the grant with you. This helps to break down the various stages of writing so that the burden is not placed on one person—you.

1. Establishing the Need

Start with a problem statement or needs assessment. Describe the current conditions at your school by using statistics that can be provided through your school or district office. The test scores are usually kept in the school or at the district office. There should be some form of reading, math, and/or science scores. The socio-economic level of the school can be ascertained by consulting the statistics on the federal lunch program at your school and a general description of the school community in your school's plan. Staff surveys can be used to compile statistics also. Community and/or parent surveys can also be used for statistical purposes. What difficulties are these current conditions causing in the classroom or school?

FINDING MONEY FOR TECHNOLOGY GRANT WRITING *(cont.)*

OK. IT IS NOW TIME TO BEGIN! *(cont.)*

2. Stating the Goal

A goal is what you are trying to achieve expressed in very general terms. Goals should be set just a little beyond the grasp, requiring extra effort and resources. In a grant proposal, the goal should be lofty. In the situation above, the goal might be that students working with technology will produce a collection of stories that will be distributed to the community through the publishing of a classroom anthology.

3. Writing the Objectives to Meet the Goal

Objectives must answer who is going to do what, when and where it will be done, and how it will be measured. State clear, measurable objectives related to the problem or need and describe a desired outcome. Keep the objectives realistic and state that you have the resources to accomplish all of your tasks within the project's time frame. **Example:** By January of 1998 the reading comprehension scores for the second grade will rise three percent. This can be measured.

4. Writing the Activities that Will be Used to Meet the Objectives

These activities indicate how the various members of the staff will work to implement the objectives as stated. The activities should be constructed so that they evolve logically from the goals and objectives. Included here are the existing resources and any plans for continuation after the funding period. This is the area that needs a "hook" to impress the grant readers so that your grant stands out from all the others, even if is being read at ten o'clock at night. A time line for implementation of the grant will most likely be called for in the grant proposal papers.

5. Evaluating the Project

How will the grant be evaluated? State who will evaluate the proposal and in what time frame. There must be clear plans for follow-up evaluation. Set the criteria for success, describe how you will gather and analyze data, and explain how results will be used to influence future activities. Describe any reports that will be produced by your project.

6. Budget

Be sure the budget reflects exactly what was stated in the objectives and action plan. Make sure the overall project cost is reasonable in relation to the project objectives. Provide as much detail as possible and include items paid for by other sources.

TIPS:

- All abbreviations must be written out first (e.g., ELD–English Language Development).
- Write simply. Visually simplify the detailed plans. Can the reader easily scan and understand your proposal?
- Include the community in the plan and in the planning.
- Substantiate all the statements in the proposal.
- Avoid using jargon.
- File your grant on time and include all the signatures requested.

A TRIP TO THE ZOO

Today zoos around the world are making an effort to design natural habitats that most closely resemble the natural environment of the animals in their care. One of the primary charges of a zoo is to work with other zoos and wildlife organizations to protect and breed rare and endangered animals.

Materials:

Animal Reference Software:

- *Zoo Keeper*
- *Jungle Safari*
- *Imagination Express: Rainforest*
- *One Small Square: Ocean*
- *How Animals Move*
- *Habitats*

- *Zurk's Learning Safari*
- *Zurk's Rainforest*
- *Zootopia*
- *The Animals! 2.0*
- *Putt-Putt Saves the Zoo*

*See list of reference materials on pages 132-166 for further program information.

Productivity Software:

- *Kid Pix* or *Kid Pix Studio*
- *Children's Writing and Publishing Center*
- *Ultimate Writing and Creativity Center*
- *Kid Works 2*

- *Storybook Weaver*
- *The Writing Center*
- *Paint, Write, and Play*

Procedure:

Into: Before the Computer

- Read several children's books on wild animals and zoos to your class. Guide the discussion to encourage students to tell about their visits to different zoos.

- Elicit responses about where animals originally resided before being brought to the zoo.

- If possible, arrange a field trip to the local zoo or invite a zoo docent to address your class.

- Select appropriate reference software and show it to your class, pinpointing the natural habitats of the animals.

- Use the blackline master page on page 55 for students to take notes on the reference software. Depending upon ability, they can write or draw the information obtained.

- Students choose animals and sketch them on paper. Depending upon ability, they then write stories about their animals.

- Decide on which productivity tool is to be used either in the lab or the classroom.

*For this example we are using *Kid Pix Studio*.

A TRIP TO THE ZOO *(cont.)*

Through: On the Computer

- Students create environments for their animals as they may appear in a zoo.

- Using their reference guide, they check that they have included all areas.

- They then place their animals in their environments, using clip art or, if not available, using the drawing tools.

- Those children who are able may then write stories about their animals.

- Students publish their work, and it can be assembled on the bulletin board or placed into classroom book form.

- Use the assessment form on page 56 for students to evaluate their publication.

Beyond: Extra Activities

- If using *Kid Pix*, students can make a title screen, a picture screen, and a text screen to assemble into a slide show. See the blackline master storyboards on pages 174 and 175. The slide shows in *Kid Pix* can be saved as stand-alone on disks and shared in other classrooms or run continuously for Open House.

- For an interesting presentation of a modern zoo, create a background on the bulletin board and have students cut and place their animals and their environments in appropriate places. Several students can group together animals that live in similar habitats.

Internet Connection:

Bill Nye the Science Guy
nyelabs.kcts.org/nyelabsZ.html

The Birmingham Zoo
http:// www.bhm.tis.net/zoo/

Take a virtual safari through the zoo.

The Electronic Zoo
http://www.netwet.wustl.edu/e-zoo.htm

Learn how veterinarians take care of animals.

National Zoological Park Home Page
http://www.si.edu/organiza/museums/zoo/homepage/nzphome.htm

Washington, DC—Visit your favorite animal and find out what goes on behind the scenes.

Rhinos and Tigers and Bears Oh My!
http://loki.ur.utk.edu/ut2kids/zoo/zoo.htmp

Find out what they eat and enjoy doing.

Zoonet
http://www.mindspring.com/~zoonet/

It provides a link to every zoo in the world.

NWF Home Page
http://www.nwf.org/nwf/

Visit the federation to find out what animals eat and you can even adopt an animal.

A TRIP TO THE ZOO *(cont.)*

ANIMAL REFERENCE NOTE-TAKING GUIDE

Directions: Draw pictures or write in the information about your animal.

Animal Name _____

Land Type	Vegetation	Foods	Other Animals Around

A TRIP TO THE ZOO *(cont.)*

Name: _____

Animal: _____

ANIMAL PROJECT EVALUATION FORM

How did I do? _____

_____

_____

Can someone tell from my project where the animal lives?   ❏ Yes   ❏ No

Can someone know what the animal eats after seeing my project?   ❏ Yes   ❏ No

Is the vegetation I show correct?   ❏ Yes   ❏ No

Do I show other animals that live alongside my animal?   ❏ Yes   ❏ No

Next time I do a project, I want to _____

_____

_____

_____

_____

_____

_____

_____

If I could do this project over again, I would _____

_____

_____

_____

_____

_____

_____

_____

A TRIP TO THE ZOO *(cont.)*

Animals in the Desert

By Marian

A TRIP TO THE ZOO *(cont.)*

In the desert animals have to look hard to find food. The hardest thing to find is water. Some animals get water from the cactus. I prefer a glass!

A TRIP TO THE ZOO *(cont.)*

Hisss! My name is Sandra. I live on the desert. It is not an easy life. All day I have to hide from the sun. I find a hole in the sand and slither into it to stay cool. At night I come out to find food. That is my favorite time.

Visit me.

by Sandra Snake

A TRIP TO THE ZOO *(cont.)*

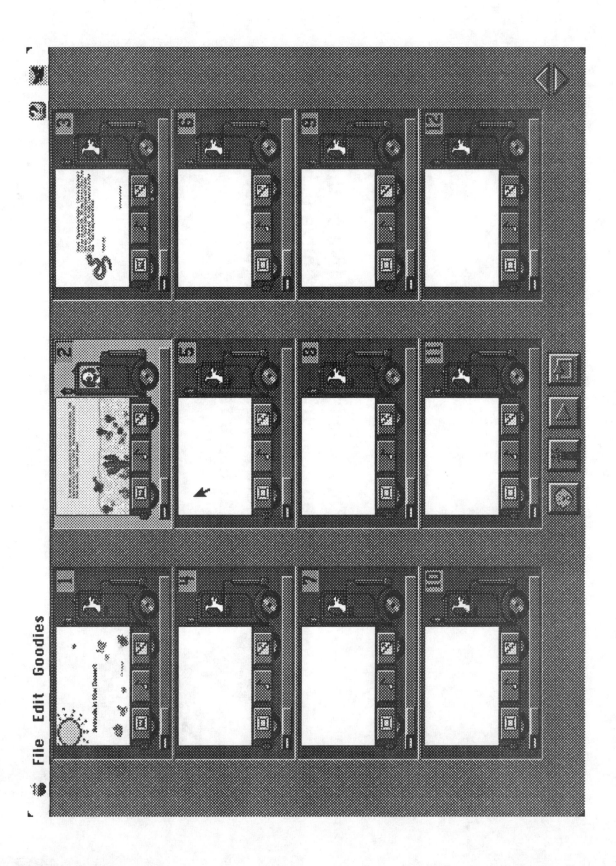

WRITING, DEVELOPING, AND PRODUCING A NUMBER SLIDE SHOW IN A SMALL GROUP

Creating a slide show is an inspiring way to introduce students to multimedia production. Working together students learn the steps involved in the development of a multimedia project. They learn to use a storyboard, set goals, work together as a team, and adhere to a schedule.

FORMING GROUPS

Groups are formed either by teacher choice or at random. The subject of the slide show is discussed in a whole-class situation, and then the groups meet on their own.

Telling the Story

- Groups brainstorm on the content of their stories.

- With one group member acting as a scribe, they then write the story.

- Now the story needs to be charted on a storyboard so that the sequence of the story and the graphics needed are organized. You could have each student do an individual storyboard or provide a large piece of butcher paper that can be used as a group storyboard.

Assigning Tasks Within a Group

- When the storyboard is completed, the group assigns tasks for production. There needs to be an artist or artists who make the final decision on the graphics and eventually place them on the screen. The typing in of the text also needs to be assigned. Someone has to decide on the transitions and audio for the story. The group may have decided on using tapes or CDs as background music, and the appropriate music has to be obtained by the sound people. One member needs to be assigned to compile all of the scenes into one slide show.

- Another method of production is for the group to divide into smaller units so that each screen has an assigned group of producers.

- The group then is assigned a time to use the computer or computers for imputing the graphics, text, sound, transitions, etc.

Putting It All Together

One student in the group compiles all of the screens into one slide show. The group views the slide show and comments on changes to be made. In *Kid Pix* it is very easy to move slides around. Just place the mouse cursor on the middle of the moving van and holding down the mouse button, move it to another place.

Viewing the Project

- The slide show can be saved as a Stand Alone and then shown on any computer that has the same hardware as the one on which it was created.

- The slide show can also be saved as a Movie if you are using *Kid Pix Studio* and then be placed into a *Kid Pix* screen. Students present their slide shows to the class. It is great fun to have students show their projects at Back to School Night or Open House.

Pages 62–65 show an example of a slide show centering around the creation of a multimedia presentation of number relationships.

WRITING, DEVELOPING, AND PRODUCING A NUMBER SLIDE SHOW IN A SMALL GROUP *(cont.)*

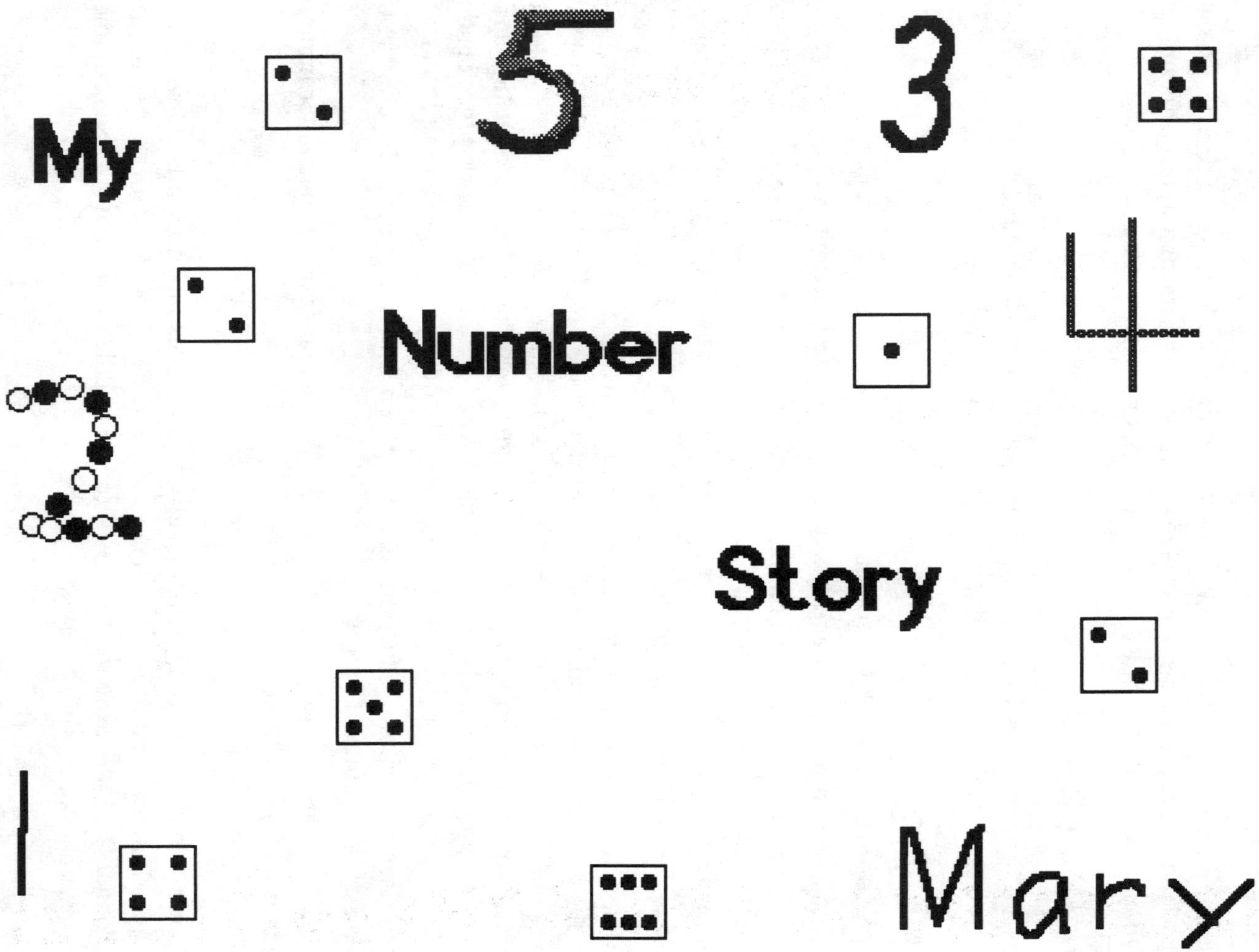

5   3

4

My Number Story

by Mary

1   2

WRITING, DEVELOPING, AND PRODUCING A NUMBER SLIDE SHOW IN A SMALL GROUP *(cont.)*

WRITING, DEVELOPING, AND PRODUCING A NUMBER SLIDE SHOW IN A SMALL GROUP *(cont.)*

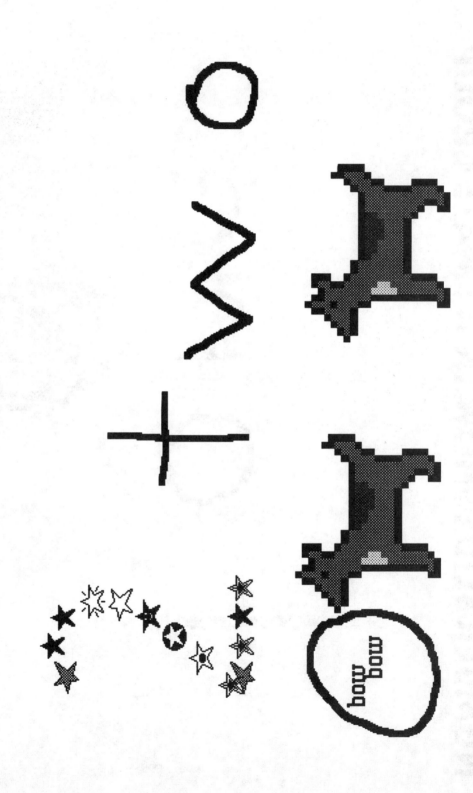

WRITING, DEVELOPING, AND PRODUCING A NUMBER SLIDE SHOW IN A SMALL GROUP *(cont.)*

3 + three

SEED SIGNS—LABELS FOR PLANTS

One of the favorite science activities in the primary classroom is planting seeds and watching and charting their growth. Students learn that it takes water and light in order for the plant to grow. They also learn that plants grow at different rates. In this project students plant their seeds in containers and make labels for their plants. They also make plant growth charts. They then note the dates that the plants reach their marked heights.

Materials:

- Plant CD
- Plants and Animals CD
- containers for plant seeds
- seeds
- planting mix
- craft sticks
- tape
- ruler

Productivity Programs:

- *Kid Pix* or *Kid Pix Studio*
- *Ultimate Writing and Creativity Center*

Procedure:

Into: Before the Computer

- Use some of the wonderful children's books available today to explore plant life with your students.
- Give each child a container, some planting mix, and some seeds.
- Students plant their seeds, water them, and place them in an area that receives light. For this example we used *Kid Pix Studio*.

Through: On the Computer

- Students design frames for their labels that suggest what is planted.
- They write the names of their seeds on the labels along with their names.
- They print them in the smallest size, if possible.
- After printing, they cut the labels and affix them to craft sticks or other small holders by taping them on the backs.

SEED SIGNS—LABELS FOR PLANTS (cont.)

To Make a Plant Growth Chart

- Using the drawing tools of the computer program, students draw stems, leaves, and roots.

- They draw straight lines at various intervals from the stems. These lines will be used to measure the progress of the plants.

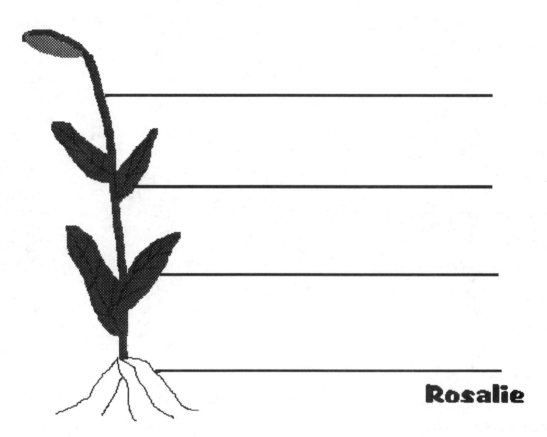

Beyond: Extra Activities

- Measure every few days and record the growth rate on the plant growth chart.

- As time passes, students use their plant charts to note the days on which the plants reached specific points.

- At the end of a month, the student created charts are displayed to note differences in growth rate of plants.

- After the plants have reached a sturdy growth, plant them in the ground in the school garden.

Internet Connections:

Yahoo! is an excellent place to begin exploring the Internet. Use the search word science. Narrow the search by typing in plants.

http://yahoo.com

SEED SIGNS—LABELS FOR PLANTS *(cont.)*

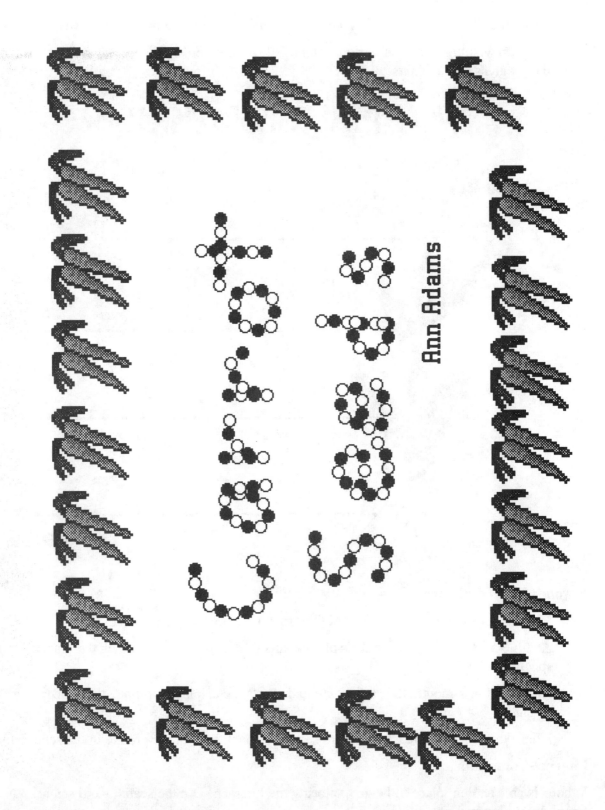

SEED SIGNS—LABELS FOR PLANTS *(cont.)*

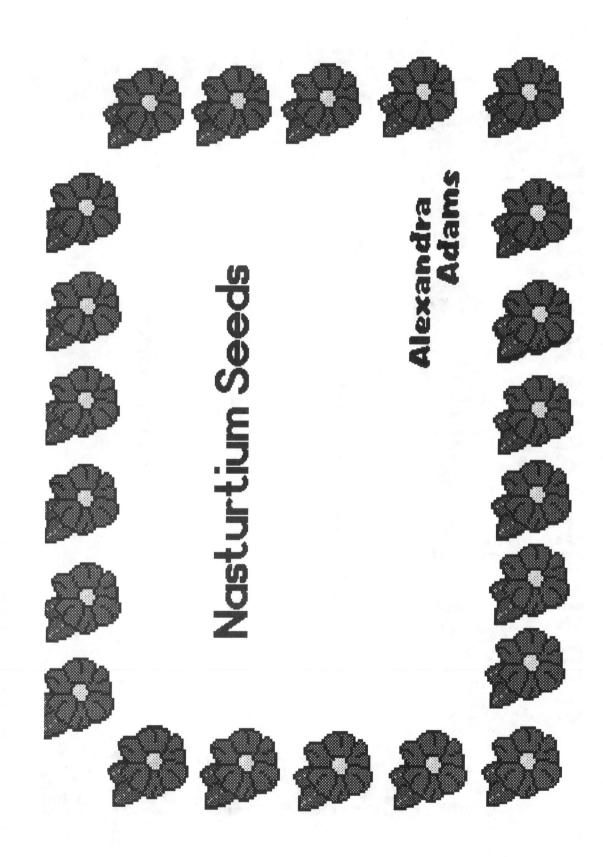

Nasturtium Seeds

Alexandra Adams

© *Teacher Created Materials, Inc.*   69   *#933 Integrating Technology into the Curriculum*

SEED SIGNS—LABELS FOR PLANTS *(cont.)*

Radish Seeds

Tommy Sanchez

SEED SIGNS—LABELS FOR PLANTS *(cont.)*

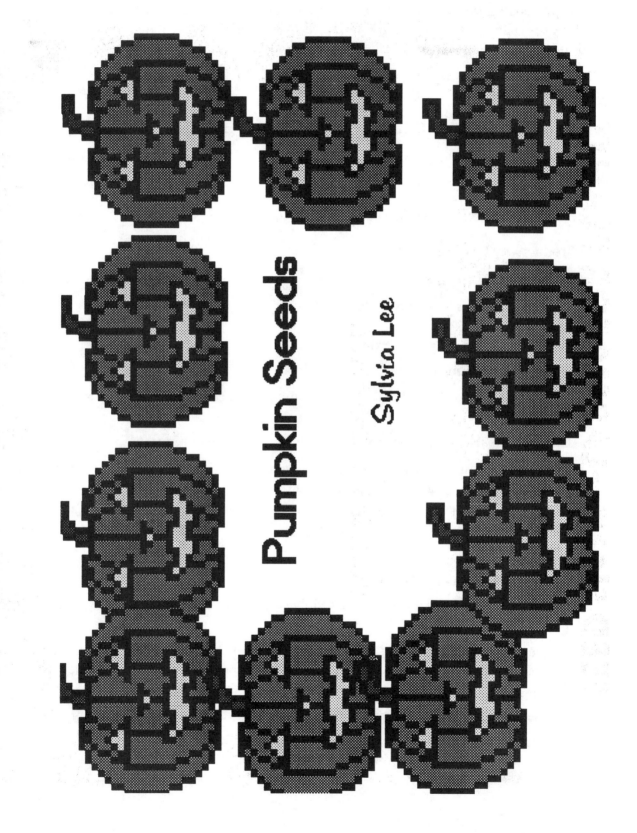

Pumpkin Seeds

Sylvia Lee

EXPLORING THE RAIN FOREST

Rain forests are the home to the majority of the plant and animal species of the world. These forests also help to control the climate and water cycles of the world. The cover formed by the tree tops in the rain forest is called a canopy. It is 100 to 200 feet (30 to 60 m) above the ground and is home to two thirds of the plants and animals living in the rain forest. The main job of the canopy is to catch the sunlight and change it into food for the trees through photosynthesis.

Materials:

Rain Forest Reference Software:

- *STV Rain Forest* laserdisc
- *Explorapedia: The World of Nature* CD
- *Rain Forest Explorer*
- Rain Forest CD

*Refer to list of reference materials on pages 132–166 for more programs.

Productivity Programs:

- *Kid Pix* or *Kid Pix Studio*
- *Ultimate Writing and Creativity Center*
- *Imagination Express: Rain Forest*
- *Storybook Weaver*

Procedure:

Into: Before the Computer

- Use children's books to aid in the understanding of the concept of the rain forest and its importance.

- Discuss with students reasons for the disappearance of the rain forest.

- Locate on a classroom map some of the locations of the rain forests. Point out the location of the Amazon, the largest remaining rain forest in the world.

- Use the "Fact Book" section of *Imagination Express: Rain Forest* to research with your class the plants, animals, and peoples of the rain forest.

- If possible view some of the rain forest reference materials as listed above, showing the vegetation and configuration of the rain forest.

- As the reference material is being viewed by students, have them use the blackline master Note-Taking Guide on page 75.

- Students sketch the rain forest, including the two levels—canopy and jungle. If there has been previous information presented on the animals and people of the rain forest, students add them to their sketches. If appropriate, have them write about their pictures.

- Decide on which of the productivity tools to use for the on-screen presentation of the rain forest.

*For this example we are using *Imagination Express: Rain Forest*.

EXPLORING THE RAIN FOREST *(cont.)*

Through: On the Computer

- Students browse through the "Fact Book" in the *Imagination Express: Rain Forest* program. They focus on subjects of interest to them as shown in their sketches and stories.

- They then choose an appropriate background and from the "stickers" available with the program, choose animals, people, and vegetation for their picture.

- If appropriate, students choose the text tool and write about their pictures. The program also allows recordings to be made.

- When finished, the pictures are printed and displayed.

Beyond: Extra Activities

- This activity is very easily done in a cooperative group setting. One student works on the research, one on the design of the page, one on the inputting of text, and one on the presentation to the class.

- Some students might like to construct with different kinds of paper the levels of the rain forest either on the bulletin board or on a temoorary display area.

- More capable students might want to research foods and medications that come from the rain forest, either using computer programs or print material.

Internet Connections:

Rainforest Action Network Home Page, the Kids Corner

http://www.ran.org/ran/kids_action/index.html

Find information about the rain forest with pictures of animals and people that live there.

National Geographic Online

http://www.nationalgeographic.com

Exploratorium

http://www.exploratorium.edu

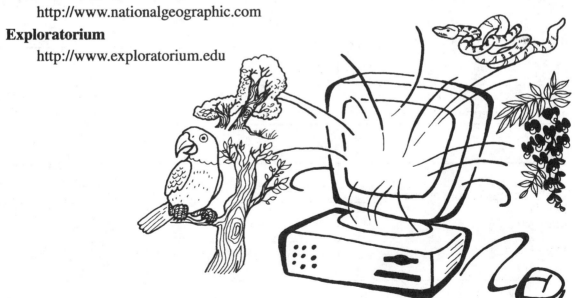

EXPLORING THE RAIN FOREST *(cont.)*

RAIN FOREST PROJECT EVALUATION FORM

Name_____

How did I do? _____

_____

_____

_____

_____

Do I understand the different levels of the rain forest?   ❑ Yes   ❑ No

What are the different levels called? _____

_____

_____

Does my picture show a good view of the rain forest?   ❑ Yes   ❑ No

What interested me most about this project was _____

_____

_____

_____

I would like to learn more about _____

_____

_____

_____

EXPLORING THE RAIN FOREST *(cont.)*

RAIN FOREST NOTE-TAKING GUIDE

Name_____

Directions: Draw or write what you see in the correct spaces. This will help you remember what you learned from viewing the reference materials.

Plants	Animals
Insects	**People**

EXPLORING THE RAIN FOREST (cont.)

IN THIS CHAPTER:

- Agouti
- Anteater
- Armadillo
- Bat
- Capuchin Monkey
- Coati
- Howler Monkey
- Jaguar
- Kinkajou
- Margay
- Mouse Opossum
- Owl Monkey
- Paca
- Peccary
- River Otter
- Sloth
- Spider Monkey
- Tapir
- Vampire Bat

MAMMALS

EXPLORING THE RAIN FOREST *(cont.)*

EXPLORING THE RAIN FOREST *(cont.)*

These are some of the animals that live in the rain forest.

THE MAGIC RAINBOW STORY

When young children begin writing creative stories, one of the important things that we as teachers work on with them is how to structure a story. At this primary age, knowing that a story has a structure of a beginning, a middle, and an end is sufficient for creative writing. In the prewriting phase, students work on establishing the place of characters in their stories along with giving some personality to the characters. For more advanced students, it would be good to discuss conflict within a simple story and how part of the story relates to how the conflict is resolved. In this project children are given a skeleton situation and are asked to enlarge on the premise to create a slide show. They do their initial planning and then elaborate, using a productivity program.

Materials:

Interactive CD-ROM Based Stories:

- *Grandma and Me*
- *Pocahontas*
- *The Little Samurai*
- *Little Monster at School*
- *Adventures of Peter Rabbit and Benjamin Bunny*
- *Mike Mulligan and His Steam Shovel*
- *The Cat Came Back*

Productivity Programs:

- *Kid Pix* or *Kid Pix Studio*
- *Kid Works 2* or *Kid Works Deluxe*
- *Storybook Weaver* or *Storybook Weaver Deluxe*
- *Ultimate Writing and Creativity Center*
- *The Writing Center*

Procedure:

Into: Before the Computer

- After reading your students a well-written children's story, review the basic structure of a story. You may want to chart the beginning, middle, and end on the board.

- List the main characters from the story.

- In a small group or, if possible, with a large projection device, view an interactive story from a CD-ROM. Have students list the characters and story sequence.

- Have students use the Magic Rainbow Planning Sheet to plan stories that they will write and illustrate using a computer.

- Use printouts of the programs graphics for the students to use in their selections to save time at the computer.

*For this example we used *Kid Pix*.

 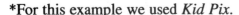

THE MAGIC RAINBOW STORY *(cont.)*

Through: On the Computer

- Have students use their planning sheets for guides as they input stories and illustrate them.

- You may want to use this project as a cooperative group activity.

- If you are using *Kid Pix*, have students use the slide show storyboard blackline master to plan their stories into slide shows.

Beyond: Extra Activities

- Assemble the pages of the students' stories into classroom books.

- Make a clamped book by stacking the pages of the book and putting a sheet of colored construction paper on the front and back and clamping it together with a binder clip.

- Use a clear vinyl report cover with a hard plastic spine to hold the pages of the book.

- Another book type could be the accordion book where the pages are mounted in sequence and taped together.

THE MAGIC RAINBOW STORY *(cont.)*

THE MAGIC RAINBOW PLANNING SHEET

Directions: Plan a story about a magic rainbow and what happens to people who see the rainbow.

Title of Your Story _____

Characters in Your Story _____

	Names	What They Look Like
1.	_____	_____
2.	_____	_____
3.	_____	_____
4.	_____	_____

How does your story begin?

_____

_____

_____

What happens in the middle of your story? What happens to the characters in your story?

_____

_____

_____

_____

_____

How does the story end? What happens to your characters at the end of your story?

_____

_____

_____

_____

_____

THE MAGIC RAINBOW STORY *(cont.)*

The Magic Rainbow

by Gregory

82

THE MAGIC RAINBOW STORY *(cont.)*

I was walking along down the street on my way home from school, when I saw a rainbow. My teacher said we could wish on a rainbow.

I made a wish.

THE MAGIC RAINBOW STORY *(cont.)*

I followed the rainbow to the end and there was my wish, a dog.

THE MAGIC RAINBOW STORY *(cont.)*

The dog followed me home and my Mom said he could stay. She must have seen the rainbow too.

THE MAGIC RAINBOW STORY *(cont.)*

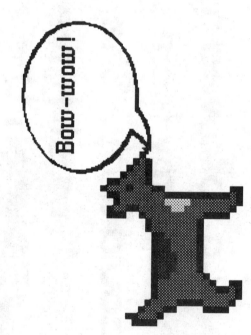

The End

THE MAGIC RAINBOW STORY *(cont.)*

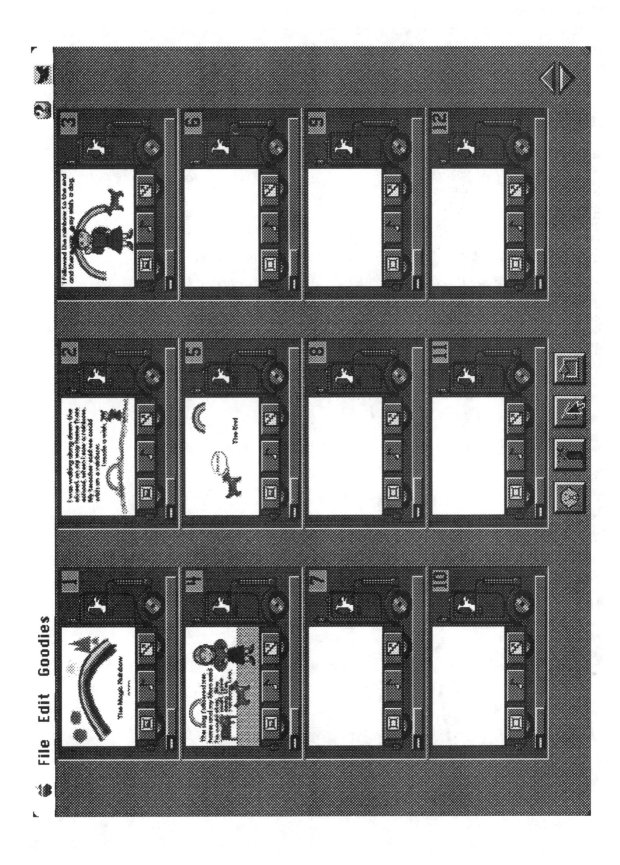

NUMBERS! NUMBERS! NUMBERS!

Many children start kindergarten knowing the number symbol, but the corresponding one-to-one relationship and the number word is learned in the school setting. To augment the discovery and directed lessons related to one-to-one relationships and number words, this project reinforces the concept taught in the classroom. Students use a productivity program to produce their own numbers book. Refer to page 91 for a printout of a student-created slide show.

Materials:

Math Reference Software:

- *Kid's Time Deluxe*
- *At Home with Stickybear*
- *Playroom*
- *Math Rabbit*
- *How Many Bugs in a Box*
- *Stickybear's Math Town*

- *Stickybear Early Learning Activities*
- *Jumpstart Kindergarten*
- *Millie's Math House*
- *Sesame Street Numbers*
- *Math Blaster Jr.*
- *Realia*

Flannelboard and appropriate objects

Productivity Programs:

- *Kid Pix* or *Kid Pix Studio*
- *Kid Works 2* or *Kid Works Deluxe*
- *Flying Colors*
- *Amazing Writing Machine*

Procedure:

Into: Before the Computer

- Use objects in the classroom environment to illustrate one object to the number 1, etc.

- Flannelboard stories and manipulatives are used to show concepts in a concrete manner.

NUMBERS! NUMBERS! NUMBERS! *(cont.)*

Into: Before the Computer *(cont.)*

- Show the computer programs to your class and to small groups and have students show on the screen the concepts of one-to-one matching.

- After students have mastered the one-to-one relationship concept, the number word might be introduced. Use flashcards, a teacher-produced slide show, and use any other way that works.

- If you are using a productivity program new to your students, you need to introduce it to the whole class or in small groups.

- Use the planning sheet on page 90 for this project.

*For this example we are using *Kid Works 2*.

Through: On the Computer

- Students use their planning sheets to create their number projects.

- They enter a number, the number word, and the picture, one for each line.

- If students have the ability, they can continue their number books past the number 10.

- Depending upon ability, they might write stories utilizing the numbers.

- Have students print their number stories.

Beyond: Extra Activities

- Mount the printouts on heavy paper.

- Student cut the number words, the objects, and the symbols apart. The pieces are then placed in envelopes and become their own number games. This makes a great sponge activity.

Internet Connections:

Ask Dr. Math

http://www.forum.swarthmore.edu/dr.math/dr-math.html

It tells how mom and dad can understand your homework.

Math Magic

http://www. forum.swarthmore.edu/mathmagic/

Work math puzzles, and you can join a team of kids around the Net to help you.

Blue Dog Can Count

http://kao.ini.cmu.edu:5550/bdf.html

He will help solve your math problems for you. Listen while Blue Dog barks out the answers to your problems.

NUMBERS! NUMBERS! NUMBERS! *(cont.)*

PLANNING SHEET

Name: _____

Number	Number Word	Number Picture

NUMBERS! NUMBERS! NUMBERS! *(cont.)*

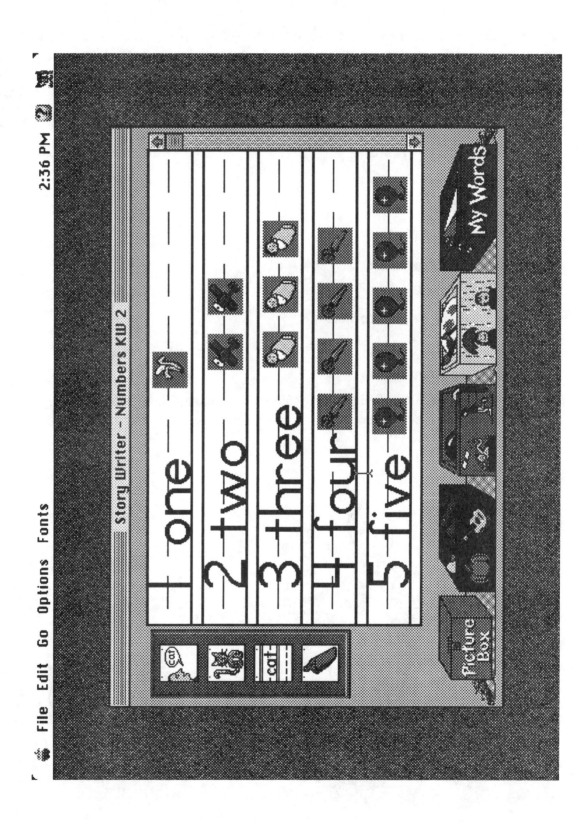

NUMBER STORIES ARE ALL AROUND US!

Number facts have much more meaning when they can be placed in context. Students writing their own number stories reinforce math concepts. In this activity students write stories involving math operations and add hints to the stories, so that other students can solve the problems. Placing these student-written stories in a folder for viewing creates a unique math text.

Materials:

Math Related Software:

- *Stickybear Math Town*
- *Zoo Zillions*
- *Interactive Math Journey*

- *Number Maze Challenge*
- *Mathville*
- *Treasure Galaxy*

Productivity Programs:

- *Storybook Weaver*
- *Amazing Writing Machine*

- *Kid Pix* or *Kid Pix Studio*

Procedure:

Into: Before the Computer

- Have your students create math problems using students in the class for props (e.g., move six students to one part of the room and move three to another part of the room to illustrate subtraction).

NUMBER STORIES ARE ALL AROUND US! *(cont.)*

Into: Before the Computer *(cont.)*

- Next have students create math problems using objects in the classroom.

- While students are creating the math problems with props, have them orally tell what they are doing.

- Use some of the computer programs listed above to reinforce the concept of story problems.

- Have students use the planning sheet on page 94 before they have their computer turns.

*For this example we have used *Storybook Weaver*.

Through: At the Computer

- Using their planning sheets, students illustrate number stories on the screen.

- They then write their number stories along with their hints.

- Students print their stories, and they are then assembled into a classroom math book.

Beyond: Extra Activities

- Place the printouts on the bulletin board and number each one.

- Place a post-it note over the hint in each problem.

- Students take pieces of paper and number them. They read the problems on the bulletin board and record their answers appropriately. When everyone has had a turn, see how many students got all the answers correct. It might be interesting for students to write the number problems along with their answers.

Internet Connections:

Ask Dr. Math

http://www.forum.swarthmore.edu/dr.math/dr-math.html

This explains how mom and dad can understand your homework.

Math Magic

http://www. forum.swarthmore.edu/mathmagic/

Solve math puzzles, and you can join a team of kids around the Net to help you.

Blue Dog Can Count

http://kao.ini.cmu.edu:5550/vdf.html

He will help solve your math problems for you. Listen while Blue Dog barks out the answers to your problems.

NUMBER STORIES ARE ALL AROUND US! *(cont.)*

NUMBER STORY PLANNING SHEET

Name: _____

Think of a time when you need to use a number operation to solve a problem. Is it during a game on the schoolyard? Is it when you go to the store to buy something? Is it when you play a game at home?

Draw your number story here.

[drawing box]

Write about your number story.

_____

_____

_____

_____

_____

Give someone a hint about how to solve your number story.

_____

NUMBER STORIES ARE ALL AROUND US! *(cont.)*

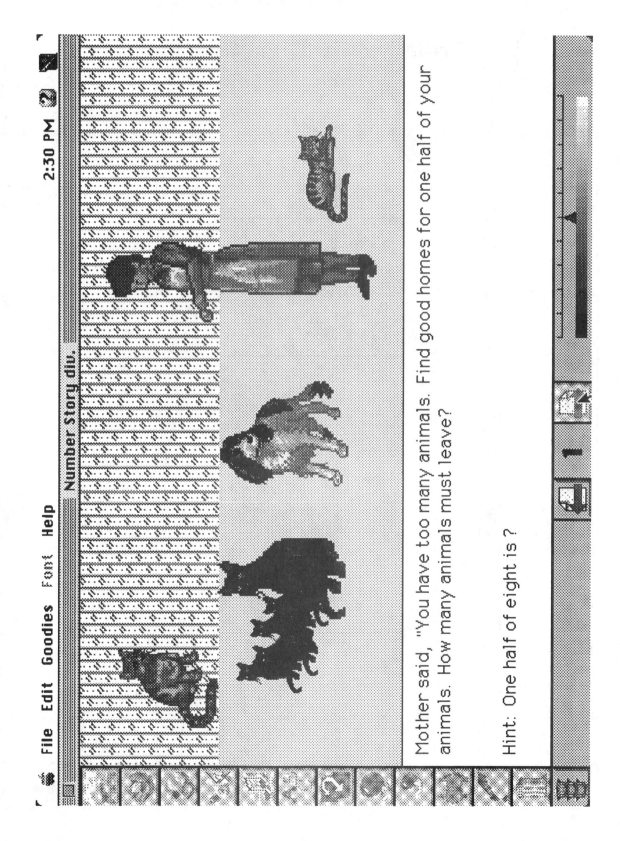

File Edit Goodies Font Help   2:30 PM

Number Story div.

Mother said, "You have too many animals. Find good homes for one half of your animals. How many animals must leave?

Hint: One half of eight is ?

NUMBER STORIES ARE ALL AROUND US! *(cont.)*

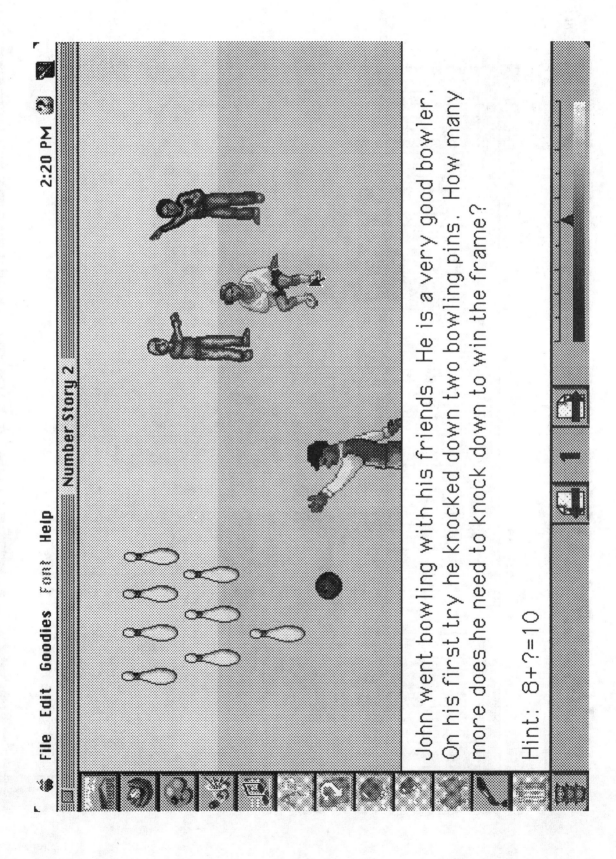

File   Edit   Goodies   Font   Help

Number Story 2

2:20 PM

John went bowling with his friends. He is a very good bowler. On his first try he knocked down two bowling pins. How many more does he need to knock down to win the frame?

Hint: 8+?=10

NUMBER STORIES ARE ALL AROUND US! *(cont.)*

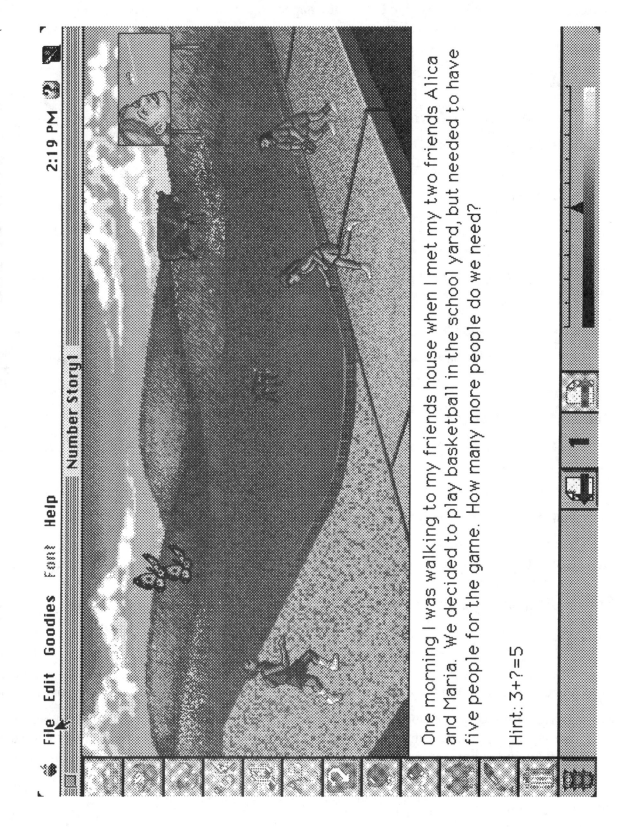

File Edit Goodies Font Help

2:19 PM

Number Story 1

One morning I was walking to my friends house when I met my two friends Alica and Maria. We decided to play basketball in the school yard, but needed to have five people for the game. How many more people do we need?

Hint: 3+?=5

WRITE WITH SYMBOLS

Native Americans long ago did not have a written alphabet; instead, they used symbols to write messages. They used pictures to tell about the happenings in their daily lives. Mainly the symbols told about events in nature. This project has students using their imaginations to create symbols that represent what they want to convey to someone else.

Materials:

Native American Reference Software

- *Native American* CD-ROM

- *Pocahontas* CD-ROM

- *Native American: Indians of the Plains* laserdisc

Productivity Programs:

- *Kid Pix* or *Kid Pix Studio*

- *Kid Works 2*

- *Flying Colors*

- *Amazing Writing Machine*

Procedure:

Into: Before the Computer

- Lead a class discussion on how people communicate with each other—language, both written and oral, body movement, and the arts.

- Write the following sentence on the chalkboard: The dad took his son fishing down by the lake.

- Ask one of your students to read the sentence.

- Now ask another student to draw the sentence on the board. Encourage the student to use a symbol for a word when possible. Ask other students to show how they would draw the symbols for the words.

- Explain that the Native Americans of long ago communicated by using symbols and sign language because they did not all speak the same language, and they did not all have a written language.

- Share some of the suggested software with your class to help them learn more about the Native Americans. Much of the software shows some of the pictographs used by the Native Americans.

- Explain to students that they are going to write a sentence using symbols. They are also going to use an ancient Native American custom of signing their picture stories by placing their handprints on them instead of their names.

- Students write their picture stories before they use the computer.

*For this example we are using *Kid Pix*.

WRITE WITH SYMBOLS *(cont.)*

Through: At the Computer

- Students choose clear screens and use the drawing tool to draw their symbols.

- If they have the ability, they can write the meanings of the words under the symbols.

- As a final step, students put their hands on the screens in the lower corners and trace around them with the drawing tool.

- If the program that you are using has a fill capability, have students choose the fill tool and colors for their hands and fill them in.

- Have them print their symbol pages and assemble them into a book, if desired. You might also want to mount them on the bulletin board for classroom display.

Beyond: Extra Activities

- To further extend the Native American experience, use clay or papier-mâché and have students "carve" their symbols.

- To simulate animal skins, brown paper bags can be crumpled in water and when dried, smoothed out and then written on with a marking pen.

Internet Connections:

A Guide to the Great Sioux Nation

http://www.state.sd.us/state/executive/tourism/sioux/sioux.htm

Learn about the languages and legends of the Sioux Nation.

Indian Lore Galore

http://www.paramount.com/ILore.html

Learn about the five Iroquois nations.

National Museum of the Native American Indian

http://www.si.edu/organiza/museums/amerind/nmai/start.htm

View artifacts of the Native American culture through exhibits of clothing, baskets, beadworks, and other objects.

Native Web Homepage

http://web.maxwell.syr.edu/nativeweb/

Learn about the Native Americans—their powwows, celebrations, etc.

OTAs Native American Resource Page

http://www.ota.gov/nativea.html

Find links to Native American music, arts, languages, and tribal governments.

Pueblo Cultural Center

http://www.hanksville.phast.umas.edu/defs/independent/PCC/pcc.html#toc

WRITE WITH SYMBOLS *(cont.)*

WRITE WITH SYMBOLS PLANNING SHEET

Name_____

Directions: Write a word and then create a symbol for that word in the spaces below.

Word	Symbol

WRITE WITH SYMBOLS *(cont.)*

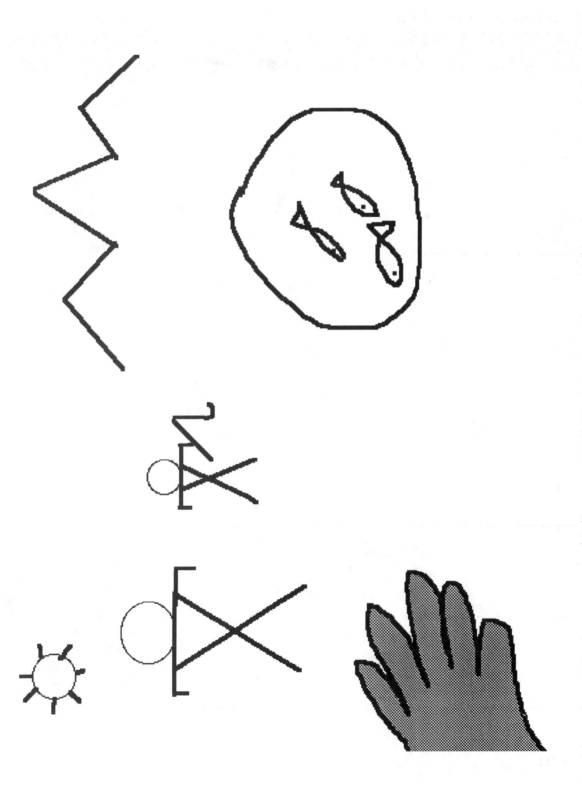

WRITE WITH SYMBOLS *(cont.)*

Today we go fishing Bradley

A BOOK ABOUT THE COMMUNITY

Within the average classroom there are multilevels of reading abilities. How does the educator meet the needs of all the children in his/her class in a subject area such as social science? The books provided by the various school districts are often on a reading level which is not necessarily the level of your class. Using technology, the teacher has a new source of reading materials. It is extremely easy to write small books on various subjects using any of several productivity programs that have graphics and text capabilities. In this project you will create a book for your students in the area of social science. Your book will include graphics and text that is on the level your students need with appropriate vocabulary.

Materials:

Community Related Software:

- *Imagination Express: Neighborhood*
- *Community Exploration*

Productivity Programs:

- *The Writing Center* or *The Bilingual Writing Center*
- *Kid Pix* or *Kid Pix Studio*
- *Storybook Weaver* or *Storybook Weaver Deluxe*
- *Imagination Express: Neighborhood*
- *ClarisWorks*
- clip art programs

Procedure:

Into: Before the Computer

- Decide which community buildings and services you want to feature.
- Review several of the programs suggested to find one that most suits your needs and ability.
- Use the planning sheet for this activity on page 104 to plan your book.

*For this example we used *The Writing Center*.

Through: On the Computer

- After booting the program, decide on the format you want. Is it two book pages to a sheet of paper to be cut apart and assembled? Is it an 8.5" x 11" (22 cm x 28 cm) sheet of paper for each book page?
- For each page of your book, enter the graphics first and then the story. You need to decide whether you are going to print in black and white and have the students add the color or print in color, if you have the capability.
- Be sure to use Print Preview or Page Preview to see how the page will look when it is printed.
- Save and print your pages.

Beyond: Extra Activities

- Assemble the pages into book form and staple together.
- Let students make a cover for each book using construction paper or heavy butcher paper.

Internet Connections:

Classroom Connect Classroom Web

http://www.classroom.net/classweb/default.htm

One of the best teacher sites on the Net, it has everything you can use for lessons.

A BOOK ABOUT THE COMMUNITY *(cont.)*

COMMUNITY BOOK PLANNING SHEET

A BOOK ABOUT THE COMMUNITY *(cont.)*

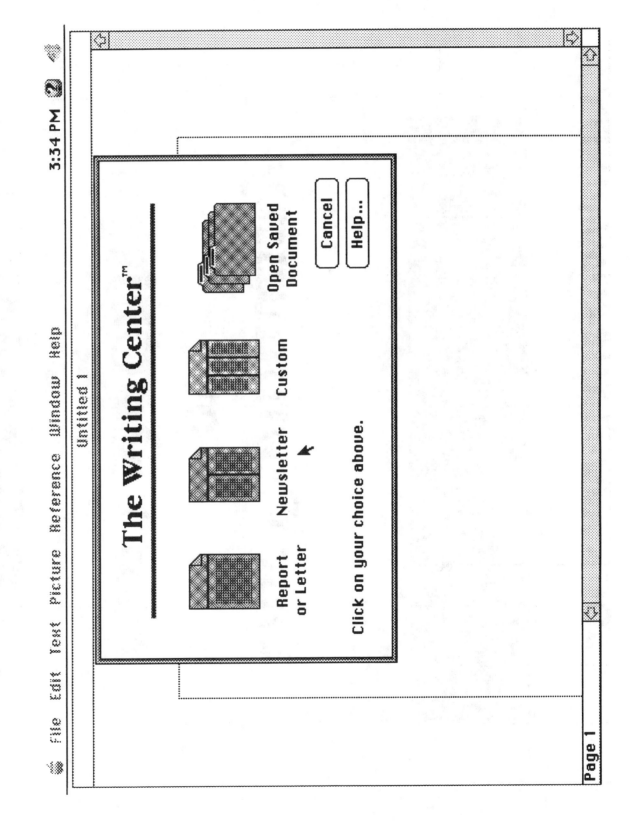

A BOOK ABOUT THE COMMUNITY *(cont.)*

Our Community of San Luis Obispo

A BOOK ABOUT THE COMMUNITY *(cont.)*
The Train

In our community we have a train station. Many people take the train to work. The man who runs the train is called the engineer.

The person who takes the tickets is called the conductor.

Our School

Our school is very big. We have many teachers and helpers. Our classroom has a computer. We learn to read, write, and do math. We also learn about other places. The principal is in charge of our school.

A BOOK ABOUT THE COMMUNITY (cont.)
The Mall

There are many stores in the mall. You can buy clothes in the

mall and you can buy a TV set. Many people work in the mall selling in the stores. You can even go to a movie in the mall.

People can buy food in the mall to eat or to take home to eat.

Apartments

There are many apartments near our school. An apartment building has many separate living places under one roof.

There are many kitchens, bedrooms, and bathrooms in an apartment house.

SHAPES ARE ALL AROUND US SLIDE SHOW

Before You Begin:

Use one of the storyboard blackline masters found on pages 174 and 175 to plan your slide show.

Create a folder on your hard drive into which you will place all the screens for your slide show. If you are using *Kid Pix Studio,* the screens are automatically saved into the KPS folder. When you are finished, you need to drag them out of that folder and put them in your own folder. It just makes life easier to work from a folder that you have labeled Slide Show Shapes.

- Create a title screen. Use the large fonts for your writing to make it clearer on the screen. Use lots of contrasting colors for your graphics.

- Use the Record option to add sound to your slides.

- Make a slide for each shape that you have taught. Don't forget to add the sound.

- After you have created each screen, save it to the hard drive. Be sure to name it so that you know what is on that screen when you go to put it in the slide show.

Making Slides:

You will see rows of three trucks with icons at the bottom. Each truck has three symbols on it: (1) Pick a Slide (it looks like a picture frame), (2) Pick a Sound (music note), and (3) the transition button.

- Click on the Pick a Slide (the first) icon. It should open your disk or folder and show you the contents of that disk or folder (all of your slides).

- Click on the slide you want and then select it. It will show a miniature version of your slide in the truck.

- Select the slides for each consecutive "truck" until all slides are in place. To quickly check the order of the slides, press the Play (like on a tape recorder) button at the bottom of the screen.

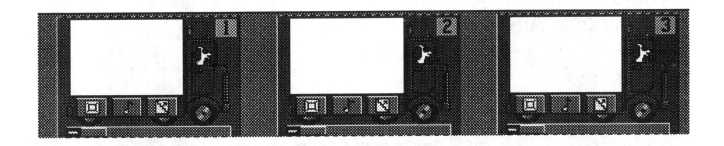

SHAPES ARE ALL AROUND US
SLIDE SHOW *(cont.)*

- Next click on the Pick a Sound button. Choose the sound you want and click Select. If you recorded in *Kid Pix*, that recording will automatically be chosen unless you tell it otherwise. If you want to record in slide show, click on the music note and then click the microphone. Record as you would in *Kid Pix*. Click on Save and then Select. You cannot have more than one sound on a slide unless you put the slide in more than one truck.

- Now choose your transition. Click on the transition button. Choose the one you want and then click Select. (The dissolve and the cut transitions are best when creating animation.)

- When you are finished, go to the File menu and select Save As. Name your slide show and click Save. (You can also save your slide show as a "StandAlone" slide show. This makes it possible to play the slide show without the *Kid Pix* application. Also, if you save it as a Quick Time movie, you can transport it into *ClarisWorks* or another application. Save it as a normal Slide Show first so that you can make changes later.)

- You can choose a background color for your slide show by going into the Goodies menu and selecting Background Color.

- To play your slide show, go to the Goodies menu and select Play Once or click the play button at the bottom of the screen. To play the slide show over and over, go to the Goodies menu and select Play Looped. This will play your slide show until the mouse is double clicked.

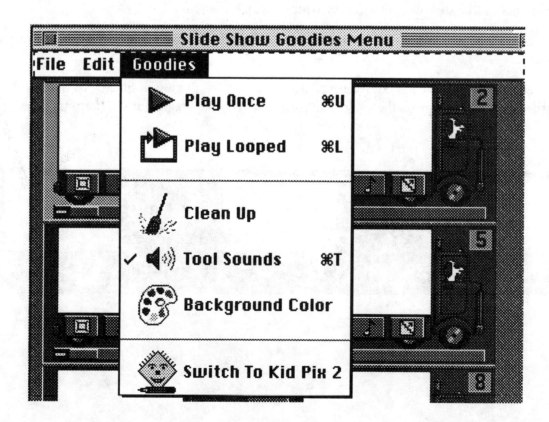

SHAPES ARE ALL AROUND US SLIDE SHOW *(cont.)*

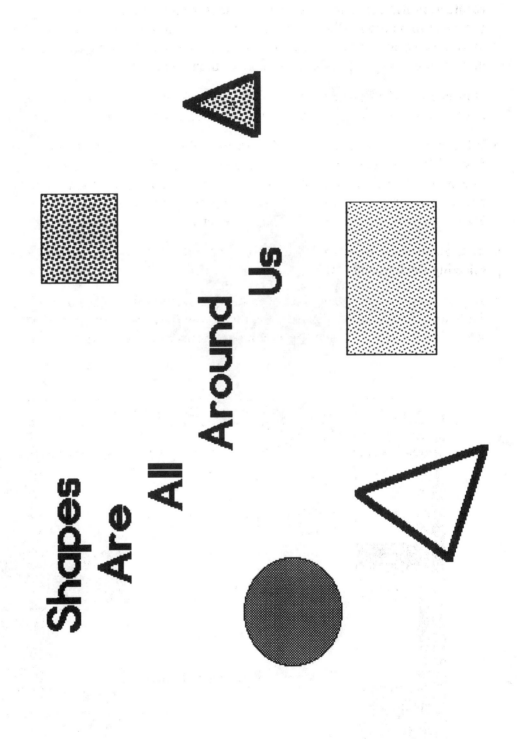

SHAPES ARE ALL AROUND US SLIDE SHOW *(cont.)*

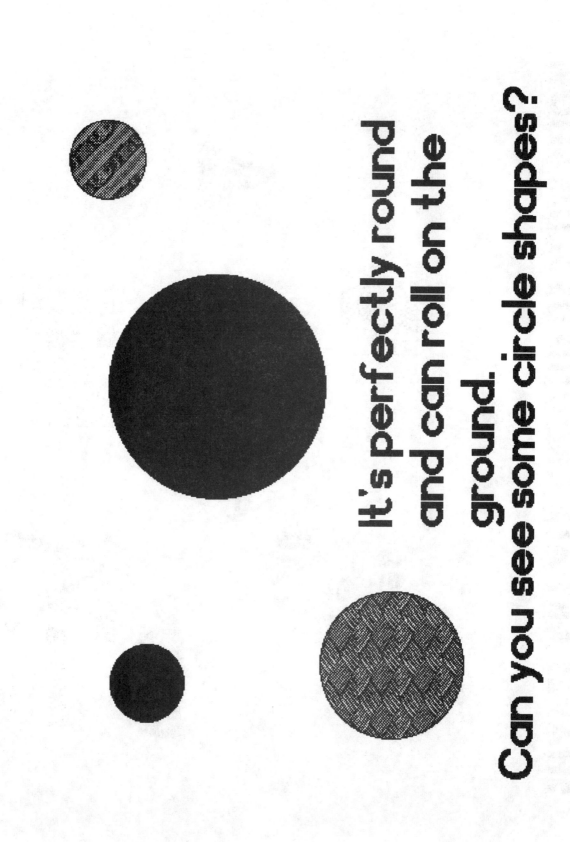

It's perfectly round and can roll on the ground.

Can you see some circle shapes?

SHAPES ARE ALL AROUND US SLIDE SHOW *(cont.)*

It doesn't roll, it doesn't hop.
4 sides the same and then you stop.

Can you see some square shapes in our classroom?

SHAPES ARE ALL AROUND US SLIDE SHOW *(cont.)*

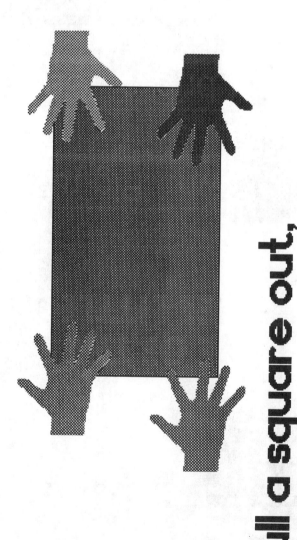

Pull a square out, and a rectangle comes about.

Can you see some rectangle shapes around you?

SHAPES ARE ALL AROUND US SLIDE SHOW *(cont.)*

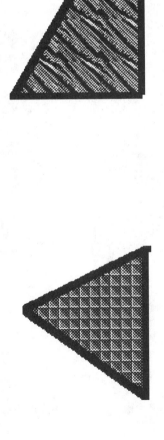

To be a triangle, you need 3 sides around.
Even if you are hanging upside down.
Can you find some triangles in our classroom?

SHAPES ARE ALL AROUND US SLIDE SHOW *(cont.)*

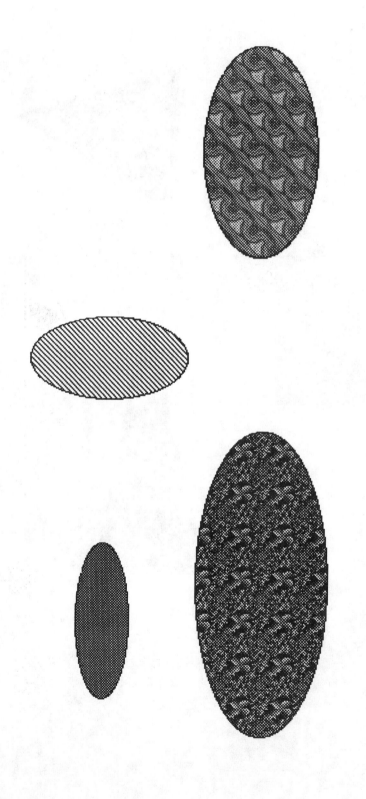

Ovals never quite get round.
They can't even roll on the ground.

Look around the room and find some oval shapes.

SHAPES ARE ALL AROUND US SLIDE SHOW *(cont.)*

We can see shapes in everything!

PICTURE IT!

Learning the parts of speech can be very difficult for young children. By using computer programs that have dramatic illustrations, it makes it visually enticing to students to learn the parts of speech. In this project which creates a story using nouns and verbs, students preplan their stories focusing on nouns and verbs, and then enter their work into a productivity program.

Materials:

Language Arts Software:

- *Kid Phonics*
- *My Words*
- *Stickybear's Reading Room*

- *Word Munchers*
- *Great Word Adventure*
- *Storybook Maker*
- *Reading Blaster Jr.*

Productivity Programs:

- *Kid Works 2* or *Kid Works Deluxe*
- *Storybook Weaver* or *Storybook Weaver Deluxe*

- *Ultimate Writing and Creativity Center*

Procedure:

Into: Before the Computer

- Review with students the place of a noun and verb in a sentence.

- Write several sentences on the board, leaving out the verbs. Ask students if they understand the meanings of the sentences.

- Using props, have students act out the sentences identifying the nouns and what happened to the nouns.

- Show to your class computer programs that emphasize the building of sentences. You may want to duplicate some sentences on sentence strips, cut them apart, and have students reassemble them in a pocket chart or along the chalkrail.

- Have students use the Picture It! planning sheet on page 120 to plot their computer projects.

*For this example we used *Kid Works Deluxe*.

Through: On the Computer

- Students input their stories into the writing area of the productivity program being used.

- If the program has the capability to change words into pictures, as do *Kid Works 2* and *Kid Works Deluxe*, have students replace the words with icons.

- Students now illustrate their stories using the capabilities of the productivity program you are using. Emphasize showing the movements of the nouns in the pictures.

- Have students print their Picture It! stories to share with their classmates.

PICTURE IT! *(cont.)*

Beyond: Extra Activities

- Arrange the printouts on the board and have students write the nouns that they used on a large piece of paper next to the stories. This way a list of nouns familiar to students is created.

- Have students read their stories to the class and choose classmates to act out their stories.

Internet Connection:

CyberKids

http://www.mtlake.com/cyberkids/

Kids create stories, articles and reviews, and artwork. There are also games to play.

Kidpub WWW Publishing

http://en-gard.com/kidpub

Kids from all over the world have their writing published on this Web site. Most of the authors include their e-mail addresses so they can be contacted.

Kids' Space

http://www.plaza.interport.net/kids-space/

Kids all over the world read stories written by kids. Many of these are in Japanese and English.

PICTURE IT! *(cont.)*

PICTURE IT! PLANNING SHEET

Name: _____

Choose a naming word. (noun)   Choose an action word. (verb)

_____   _____

Draw it here.   Draw it here.

What happened to your naming word?_____

_____

_____

Write your story here._____

_____

_____

_____

_____

_____

_____

_____

PICTURE IT! *(cont.)*

Where Did My Ball Go?

By Marian

PICTURE IT! *(cont.)*

A TIME LINE OF THE STORY OF THE THREE LITTLE PIGS

Constructing time lines showing the sequence of events, be they a day long, a year long, or several years long, helps students to learn how to collect data, enter data onto a time line, and analyze the completed time line. Many areas of the curriculum can be enhanced by the use of a time line: math, language arts, science, and social studies. This project has students constructing a time line of the sequence of events in the story of *The Three Little Pigs*. This particular project can be adapted for any stories or books your students have read.

Materials:

Children's Stories Related Software:

- *Reading Development Library Level 1*
- *There Is Tyrannosaurus Trying on Pants*
- *What Was That!*
- *Aladdin*

- *The Three Little Pigs*
- *Three Billy Goats Gruff*
- *Peter Rabbit*
- *Stellaluna*

Productivity Programs:

- *TimeLiner*
- *Kid Pix* or *Kid Pix Studio*
- any word processing program with graphics capability

Procedure:

Into: Before the Computer

- Review the story of *The Three Little Pigs* with students. Use a book, flannelboard cutouts, or a computer program.
- List the sequence of events on the chalkboard or on large paper.
- Have students use the blackline master on page 124 as a guide for the creation of their time lines.
- If you are going to use a new productivity program with students for this project, be sure to introduce it to the class.

*For this project we are using *TimeLiner*.

Through: On the Computer

- Students bring their planning sheets with them to the computer.
- If you are using *TimeLiner* with your class, enter the time of the day and the event. As they add each event and the time of day, the program places the entries into chronological order.
- If you are using *Kid Pix*, have students use the line tool to draw the bases of the time lines and use the text tool to type in the events. They can then illustrate their time lines with graphics.

Beyond: Extra Activities

- Using a program that has clip art or graphics capabilities, have students draw or use the clip art to create pictures of the different segments of the story and then print, cut, and paste on their time lines in the appropriate place.
- Make a time line of an event and use pictures that you have taken to illustrate the time line.

A TIME LINE OF THE STORY OF THE THREE LITTLE PIGS *(cont.)*

THE THREE LITTLE PIGS TIME LINE PLANNING SHEET

Directions: Draw each part of the story and write what happened. After you have filled in this planning sheet, take it with you to a computer.

Wolf meets first pig—house of straw.		Wolf meets third pig—house of bricks.	

Take this planning sheet with you to the computer.

A TIME LINE OF THE STORY OF THE THREE LITTLE PIGS *(cont.)*

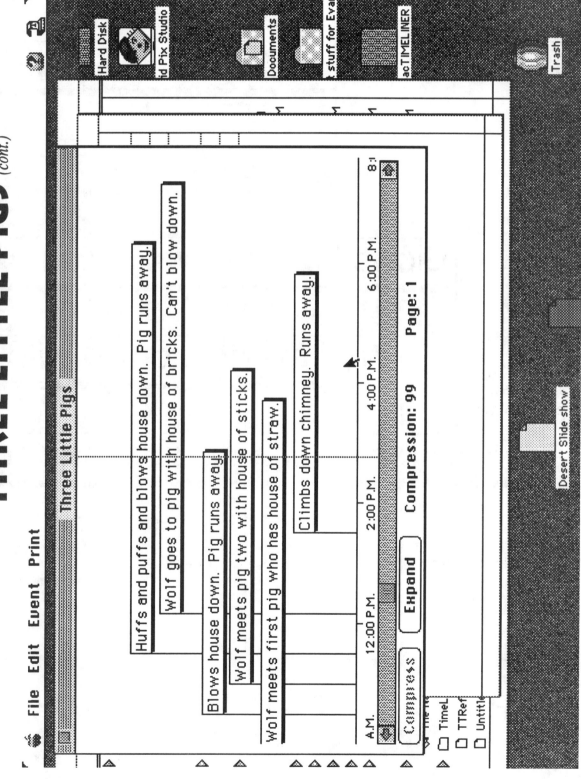

A TIME LINE OF THE STORY OF THE THREE LITTLE PIGS *(cont.)*

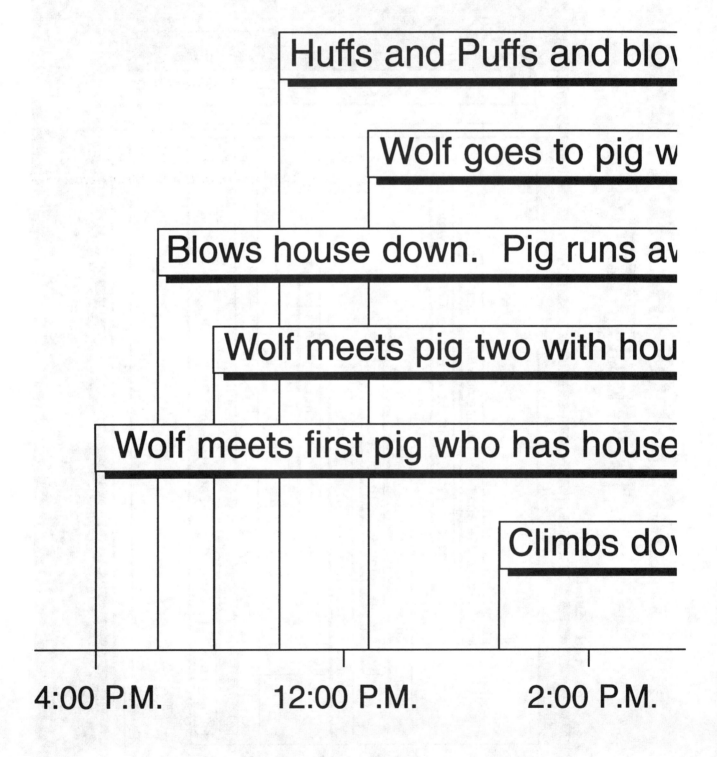

Huffs and Puffs and blo

Wolf goes to pig w

Blows house down. Pig runs a

Wolf meets pig two with hou

Wolf meets first pig who has house

Climbs do

4:00 P.M.   12:00 P.M.   2:00 P.M.

A TIME LINE OF THE STORY OF THE THREE LITTLE PIGS (cont.)

ws house down. Pig runs away.

with house of bricks. Can't blow down.

way.

se of sticks.

e of straw.

wn chimney. Runs away.

| 4:00 P.M. | 6:00 P.M. | 8:00 P.M. |

CHOOSING AND EVALUATING SOFTWARE

To truly integrate technology into the primary classroom curriculum, the teacher has to choose the software for the classroom with an eye to its integrated use. "There is so much educational software available today, how do I choose the correct one for my class," asks the primary teacher in a confused tone of voice. In the following pages we hope to alleviate that confusion by sharing the best of the primary software with you in a simplified format.

Suggestions for criteria to use when selecting software will also be offered. Included in this section are two pages of software evaluation forms you might want to use when selecting software.

CATEGORIES OF SOFTWARE

It is generally agreed that software can be divided into specific categories:

Productivity—word processing, spreadsheet, multimedia, and authoring

Tutorial—teaches material in an interactive way; decides when student has completed enough tasks to proceed

Simulation—presents situation where student takes risks as if confronted with the real-life situation

Drill and Practice—provides practice in skills students have previously been taught

Problem Solving—uses critical thinking skills; not relegated to any specific content area

Games—specific learning objectives with the game serving as a motivational device—also called edutainment

SOFTWARE SELECTION

According to Dr. Vicki Sharp in her book *Computer Education for Teachers*, there are eight steps to be used in choosing good software.

- Know the specific software needs of the population.—grade level, ability level, purpose of software, class language, needs

- Locate the software.—educational software catalogs, preview centers, magazines, demo copies from the publishers, reviews, software stores

- Research hardware compatibility.—memory requirements, hardware requirements (i.e., CD-ROM player needed)

- Examine the program's contents.—appropriateness for students, use evaluation form (page 130)

- Look at instructional design.—learner control, reinforcement, sequencing, flexibility, appearance

- Check to see how easily a program is learned.—easy to learn, simple commands, help screen

- Evaluate a program in terms of consumer value.—lab packs, site licenses

- Investigate the technical support and cost.—toll-free number for help, return policy

CHOOSING AND EVALUATING SOFTWARE *(cont.)*

EDUCATIONAL SOFTWARE PACKAGING

There are several ways in which educational software is packaged for school use:

Home Version–Consumer Version—includes one disk and no teaching materials.

School Version—includes disk and a teacher manual which usually includes online and offline classroom material for use with the program. Most have lesson plans, templates, and blackline masters.

Lab Pack—usually includes five disks and teacher classroom materials. Some lab packs are available with ten or more disks. The price makes this a good school purchase for 5, 10, or 15 computers.

Site License—means permission is granted for legally copying the program for every computer in a specific building or district. It includes teacher classroom materials and is a good choice for schools with many computers. Some site licenses are for an unlimited number of copies; however, others are for a specific number.

Network Version—indicates the program has been specifically formatted so that it can to be installed on the network and shared with all of the networked computers.

SOFTWARE EVALUATION RATING SHEET

Program Name: _____

Grade Level: _____

Subject Area: _____

	Poor		Deficient		Sufficient		Desirable		Exemplary	
Content: Alignment with curriculum	1	2	3	4	5	6	7	8	9	10
Appropriate for grade level	1	2	3	4	5	6	7	8	9	10
Accuracy	1	2	3	4	5	6	7	8	9	10
Ease of Use: Easy program loading	1	2	3	4	5	6	7	8	9	10
Simple screen directions	1	2	3	4	5	6	7	8	9	10
Program Appearance: Uncluttered screen	1	2	3	4	5	6	7	8	9	10
Material clearly presented	1	2	3	4	5	6	7	8	9	10
Learning Style: Uses more than one modality	1	2	3	4	5	6	7	8	9	10
Support: Technical support #	1	2	3	4	5	6	7	8	9	10
Teacher manual with activities	1	2	3	4	5	6	7	8	9	10

Hardware: _____   Printer compatibility: _____

Memory needed: _____   Needs hard disk? _____

Computer compatibility: _____   Peripherals needed: _____

EDUCATIONAL SOFTWARE DISTRIBUTORS

The following companies specialize in software for the school setting for grades PreK through 12. You will find their sales personnel extremely knowledgeable in helping you make you software choices. Most companies distribute catalogs and would be pleased to add you to their mailing lists.

Bytes & Pieces

(800) 338-3475

Learning Services

(800) 877-9378

Club Kidsoft

(800) 345-6150

Scranton Quality Computers

(800) 777-3642

Computer Plus

(800) 446-3713

Software Express

(800) 527-7638

Educational Resources

(800) 624-2926

SoftWareHouse

(800) 541-6078

EIS

(800) 955-5570

Sunburst Communications

(800) 321-7511

FastTrac

(800) 927-3936

The Reading & Computing Place

(800) 888-0553

LANGUAGE ARTS SOFTWARE

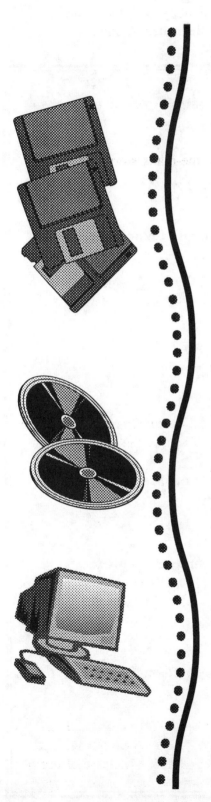

Title: *The Amazing Writing Machine*

Publisher: Brøderbund

This easy-to-use program helps students to write and illustrate their own books, journals, essays, letters, and poems. Graphics and idea generating tools are available to enhance the writing process. Using *Kid Pix*-type tools makes this an easy extension for younger students.

Title: *Arthur's Reading Race*

Publisher: Brøderbund

Arthur challenges his sister to a reading contest. Featured are animation and sound with three activities embedded in the story to enable prereaders to develop early reading skills and recognize words in various contexts.

Title: *Bailey's Book House*

Publisher: Edmark

Students learn letters, acquire vocabulary, make rhymes, and publish their own books starring Bailey and his neighborhood friends. Using the program, students can print out their own greeting cards.

Title: *Berenstain Bears Get in a Fight* CD

Publisher: Brøderbund

On a rainy day, the sister and brother bears keep clashing over everything, but Mama Bear brings the fighting to a halt. Included in the package are print editions.

Title: *Build-A-Book with Roberto*

Publisher: Theatrix

Roberto the friendly hippo, lets students make choices for him about how the story should proceed and then lets them print the story. Students can printout masks expressing various feelings along with other activities best suited for the PreK through first grade child.

LANGUAGE ARTS SOFTWARE *(cont.)*

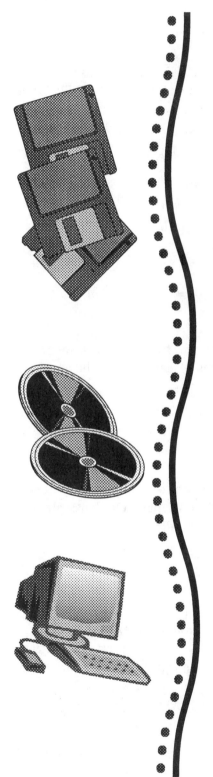

Title: *The Busy World of Richard Scarry–Best Reading Program Ever*

Publisher: Simon & Schuster

Through activities in five locations, students work on reading, writing, phonics, listening, sight word development, simple spelling and letters and sounds. There are 15 on-screen Busytown stories, and students can compose silly fill-in-the-blank stories or write their own.

Title: *Camp Frog Hollow*

Publisher: Don Johnston

K.C. and Clyde go to summer camp where students learn the vocabulary from the PreK through the third grade Dolch Sight Vocabulary.

Title: *The Cat Came Back*

Publisher: Sanctuary Woods

This interactive book allows students to follow along as the story is read to them or to read it themselves. Pictures can be turned into animation, words into songs, and questions into answers. This program is multilingual–English, Spanish, and French.

Title: *Chicka Chicka Boom Boom*

Publisher: Simon & Schuster Interactive

Based on the award-winning book of the same name, students romp through the alphabet. The program includes five activities and lots of music.

Title: *Children's Writing and Publishing Center*

Publisher: The Learning Company

The premier writing and publishing program for young students, it is available only in Apple and DOS formats. This program allows students to write, import graphics, and publish. The ease of use of this program has attracted teachers for many years. Additional packages of graphics are also available.

LANGUAGE ARTS SOFTWARE *(cont.)*

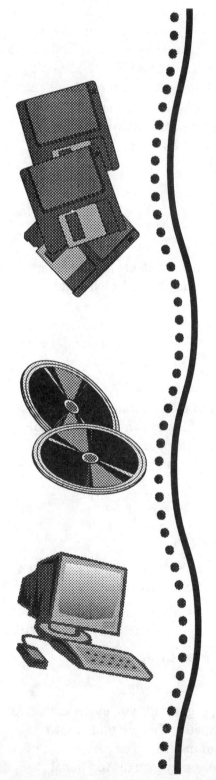

Title: *Curious George ABC Adventure*

Publisher: Houghton Mifflin Interactive

Covered are letter names and shapes, alphabetical order, basic letter phonemes, first-letter sounds, sorting by first letter, vocabulary, and listening skills.

Title: *Curious George Early Learning Adventure*

Publisher: Houghton Mifflin Interactive

Covered are color, shape, size, listening skills, pattern recognition and matching, same and different recognition, rhyming and alliteration, and mouse skills.

Title: *Dr. Peet's Picture Writer*

Publisher: Dr. Peet's Software

Click the mouse on the pictures of people, food, toys, and more. The pictures turn into talking picture words placed properly in simple sentences and print in color.

Title: *Dr. Seuss's ABC* CD

Publisher: Brøderbund

More than 400 alphabetically-inspired surprises are hidden within 26 pages. This computer program would have made Dr. Seuss proud of the way it portrays his humor, rhyme, and illustrations.

Title: *Easy Street/Spanish Easy Street*

Publisher: Mindplay

Young students walk along Easy Street to the stores of their choice to purchase items on their shopping lists. Players must complete all their shopping before returning home. Introduced are classification, labeling, discrimination skills, visual memory, problem solving, counting and matching numbers, letters, shapes, and patterns. Options include skill-level choices.

LANGUAGE ARTS SOFTWARE *(cont.)*

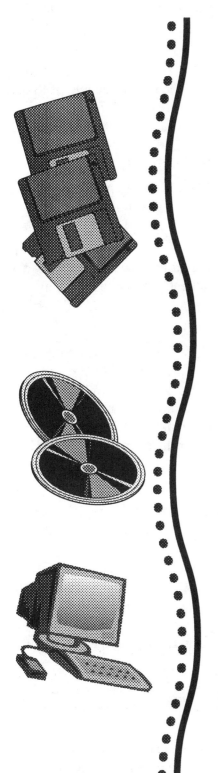

Title: *Franklin's Reading World*

Publisher: Sanctuary Woods

An engaging reading skills builder, the turtle is starred in the book series. Students explore ten scenes in Franklin's world, including the soccer field, the pond, and the woods. In each scene, students play with the word builder, the sentence builder, and the memory game.

Title: *Golden Books Series*

Publisher: Jostens Home Learning

Familiar tales for students help them learn important early reading skills. Activities include Story Reader, Story Writer, Story Thinker, Word Play, and a different Rhyme Reader story for every title.

Title: *Great Word Adventure*

Publisher: 7th Level

Students are invited to play a series of multilevel games that teach word recognition, categorization, alphabetization, compound words, rhymes, synonyms, and antonyms. Words can be added to the 2000 word database.

Title: *Green Eggs and Ham*

Publisher: Brøderbund

Dr. Seuss' best-selling classic is brought to life on the screen where students can interact as they explore the story while developing phonic and word recognition skills.

Title: *Gregory and the Hot Air Balloon*

Publisher: Brøderbund

Gregory finds himself in a quandary when he takes a ride in a hot air balloon and finds himself whisked away to a faraway land. He must explore his surroundings to solve problems.

Title: *Jo-Jo's Reading Series*

Publisher: Mindplay

Reading Castle

A discovery adventure where students learn one-syllable word families ending in three letters (e.g., ake, all, eep, and, etc.), words animate and are spoken.

LANGUAGE ARTS SOFTWARE *(cont.)*

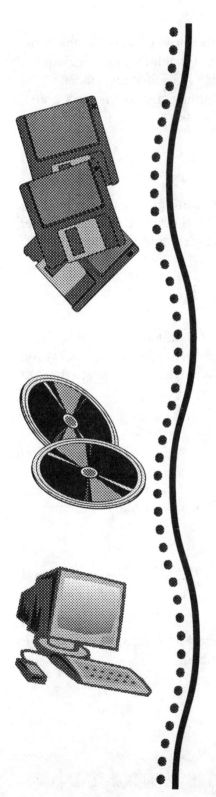

Reading Circus

Circus characters help students learn one-syllable word families ending in two letters.

Reading Ranch

An interactive program blending phonics and sight-reading of initial consonant blends, it also records students' responses for immediate feedback.

Reading River

Using one-syllable word families with three-letter endings (e.g., ent, ose, unk, and ook), words animate and are spoken.

Reading Rocket

An interactive adventure that teaches children how to learn to read diphthongs and digraphs, it records students' responses and plays them back for immediate feedback.

Title: *JumpStart First Grade* **CD**

Publisher: Knowledge Adventure

Skill-building activities include words-to-pictures games, time telling, painting, color mixing, and map making. Eight interactive storybooks with 50 illustrated stories introduce your class to world cultures, geography, and science.

Title: *JumpStart Kindergarten* **CD**

Publisher: Knowledge Adventure

This kindergarten curriculum is on a disk. There are eleven interactive learning modules with over 80 puzzles and game activities. Telling time, identifying upper and lowercase letters, rhyming words, matching shapes, understanding prepositions, recognizing numbers, and sorting objects are all included.

Title: *JumpStart Second Grade* **CD**

Publisher: Knowledge Adventure

Dozens of interactive educational modules challenge students to learn about math, science, writing, and language arts while working with CJ the frog and his sidekick Edison on a journey through 22 interactive adventures.

LANGUAGE ARTS SOFTWARE (cont.)

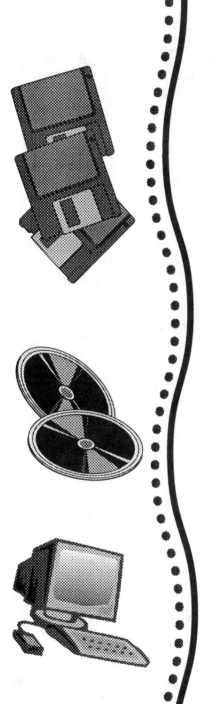

Title: *Just Grandma and Me*

Publisher: Brøderbund

Little Critter and his Grandma take the bus to the beach where each page comes alive with hot spots and text.

Title: *Just Me and My Dad*

Publisher: GT Interactive

This is Mercer Mayer's story of the adventures of Little Critter's camping trip with his dad. It includes 12 screens, each featuring 20 or more hot spots that come alive with sound effects and animation. Students hear Little Critter read the story, or they watch the video.

Title: *Kid Phonics*

Publisher: Davidson and Associates

Three exciting activities provide a multimedia learning environment that builds the auditory experience for students to progress from hearing the sounds that make up words to actually reading the words themselves. Included are digitized speech for all prompts and sounds and a construction tool that allows students to construct words phonetically and watch them turn into correctly spelled words for their dictionary.

Title: *Kid Works 2*

Publisher: Davidson and Associates

Students create and hear their very own illustrated stories. A word processor, a paint program, and text-to-speech technology are combined. The CD version hooks up to the Internet, and the program also comes in English and Spanish.

Title: *Magic Tales*

Publisher: Davidson and Associates

Three tales from Russia, Africa, and Japan are read by students, or they can have them read aloud. *Bab Yaga and the Magic Geese*, *Imo and the King* and *The Little Samurai* have music and graphics that are representative of the individual countries.

LANGUAGE ARTS SOFTWARE *(cont.)*

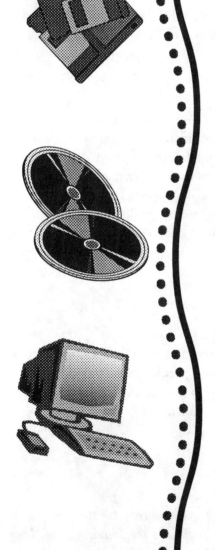

Title: *McGee Series*

Publisher: Lawrence Productions

McGee has three adventures that introduce students to manipulating the keys on the computer. There are over 30 interactive activities with no reading. The series is excellent for oral language development and includes *McGee*, *McGee at the Fun Fair*, and *McGee Visits Katie's Farm*.

Title: *Me & My World*

Publisher: The Learning Company

Introduceing vocabulary with a multimedia picture dictionary, the 18 pictures in the photo album teach students 30–45 words, many with animations.

Title: *Mike Mulligan and His Steam Shovel*

Publisher: Houghton Mifflin Interactive

The beloved story is retold in either a "Play in the Story" or "Read to Me" mode. Included are four activities: memory and matching, map reading, pattern recognition, and a tutorial on how a steam shovel works.

Title: *Mixed Up Mother Goose*

Publisher: Sierra

Students wander through an enchanted land, trying to repair the broken rhymes of Mother Goose. When a rhyme is repaired, it comes to life.

Title: *My Make Believe Castle*

Publisher: LCSI

There is an easy interface for students to use while exploring a castle and meeting its inhabitants. Each room of the castle features skill-building activities which include problem solving, critical-thinking skills, sequential planning, creativity, and memory.

LANGUAGE ARTS SOFTWARE *(cont.)*

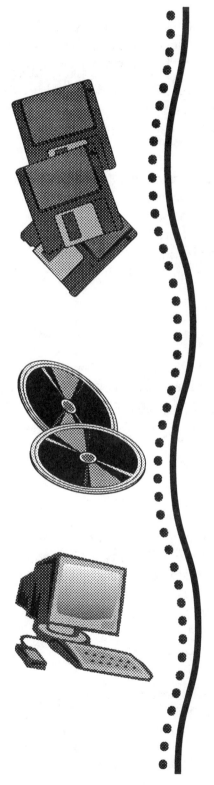

Title: *My Words*

Publisher: Hartley

Students create stories and listen to the computer read them back. They select words from a word bank and put them in their sentences. They can also hear the words in their word bank pronounced. Sounds can be added to the stories they have written. Stories can be printed.

Title: *Ocean Escape* CD

Publisher: Computer Curriculum Corporation

Five learning environments designed to help students with their development of reading skills are featured. Interactive activities have students hear words and funny sounds. The story can be read aloud and clickable words and sentences are read aloud.

Title: *Paint, Write & Play!*

Publisher: The Learning Company

An easy-to-use writing program that lets students use clip art or painting tools, sounds and animations to illustrate their writings, stories written by students are read aloud. Students build basic skills in writing and vocabulary while in a creative mode. Word lists are available to help beginning writers add words to stories without typing.

Title: *Peter Rabbit & Benjamin Bunny*

Publisher: Mindscape

Two stories, eleven skill-building activities, thirteen illustrated nursery rhymes and 200 clickable hot spots are in this beautiful traditionally illustrated program.

Title: *Pink Pete's ABC's*

Publisher: Orange Cherry

Four alphabet activities help students recognize the letters of the alphabet, their sounds, and words that begin with certain letters.

LANGUAGE ARTS SOFTWARE *(cont.)*

Title: *The Playroom*

Publisher: Brøderbund

From a playroom filled with toys, students click on toys and objects to enter activities including numbers, letters, and time. The alphabet activity has students choosing letters which turn into objects to be placed in any of three environments: farm, castle, and town.

Title: *Read, Write & Type*

Publisher: The Learning Company

Students work on their reading, phonics, and keyboarding skills with Lefty and Right Way cartoon hand characters. Students are introduced to the keyboard and the 26 storytellers who live inside it. Featured are 57 sound games with 200 word pictures, more than 600 words to type, and 84 imaginary e-mail messages from children around the world.

Title: *Reader Rabbit 1*

Publisher: The Learning Company

This classic reading program includes four animated activities which help develop fundamental reading, spelling, and thinking skills while working in Reader Rabbit's word factory. Over 200 three-letter words and more than 70 pictures provide comprehensive coverage of the early reading curriculum.

Title: *Reader Rabbit 2*

Publisher: The Learning Company

Students take a fantasy railroad trip through a word mine, vowel pond, match patch, and barnyard dance to build early reading and thinking skills. The barnyard dance is done by some chickens which, when placed in correct alphabetical order, show their dancing skills. All activities have multiple levels.

Title: *Reader Rabbit's Interactive Reading Journey* CD

Publisher: The Learning Company

Forty progressively challenging storybooks, on screen and off, build reading comprehension as students take a journey through 20 letter lands and stop at skill houses along the way to build skills that will help them read the storybooks. Over 100 lessons in phonics and word recognition provide practice in sounding out words. Included are read-to-me and read-it-myself mode. Up to 99 students can be tracked for progress.

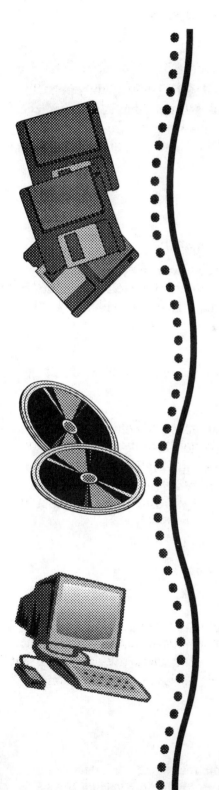

LANGUAGE ARTS SOFTWARE (cont.)

Title: *Reader Rabbit's Interactive Reading Journey 2*

Publisher: The Learning Company

Students continue the journey with increasing difficulty levels. There are 15 reading lands and numerous clickable hot spots with animation, music, sound effects, and humor. Phonic blends, vowel sounds, syllables, long and short vowel sounds, and comprehension are reinforced in this program which also has 30 interactive storybooks.

Title: *Reading Blaster Jr.*

Publisher: Davidson and Associates

Blasternaut takes students on five missions in which they learn to sound out vowels and consonants, match and identify 200 key words, and construct stories through sequencing. There are 25 printable books.

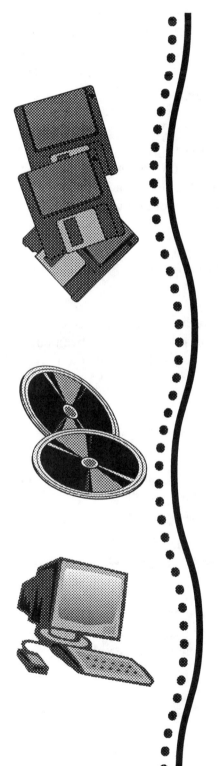

Title: *Reading Development Library Volume I and Volume II*

Publisher: The Learning Company

A series of interactive classic stories (e.g., *The Three Little Pigs, Goldilocks and the Three Bears, Jack and the Beanstalk,* and *City and Country Mouse*) use a developmental approach to building essential reading skills. Each book has been especially designed with vocabulary, grammar, font size, and reading speed targeted to specific levels of a child's reading development.

Title: *Reading Magic Series*

Publisher: Tom Snyder Productions

Flodd, the Bad Guy, Jack and the Beanstalk, Fizz & Martina in Tough Krudd, Hansel and Gretel, and *Hilary and the Beast* are the titles of this series which has a read-aloud interactive storybook that lets students choose the paths of their stories as they read along.

Title: *Reading Maze*

Publisher: Great Wave

Essential beginning reading skills are introduced through mazes where students solve picture, letter, word, and sentence problems.

LANGUAGE ARTS SOFTWARE *(cont.)*

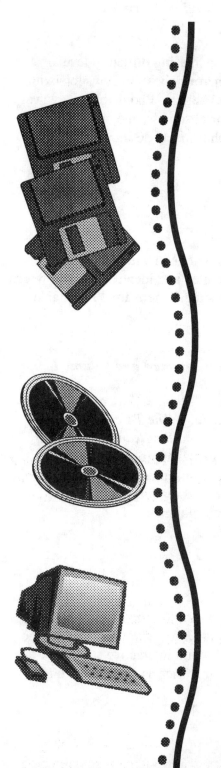

Title: *Reading Rodeo*

Publisher: Heartsoft

Students select picture of objects that begin with a particular consonant. It is also available in Spanish.

Title: *Reading Success for Kids: Aladdin*

Publisher: Pixel Genius

Students interact with Aladdin as he journeys through the ancient world. Over 300 clickable words lead to on-screen definitions and the word used in a sentence, which can be read aloud. Online activities follow each chapter of the story, reinforcing word recognition and story comprehension.

Title: *Reading Success for Kids: Pocahontas*

Publisher: Pixel Genuis

Students learn about the life of the Northeastern Native Americans through this beautifully illustrated story of Pocahontas. Each chapter is followed by activities that reinforce vocabulary acquisition and comprehension.

Title: *Rhyme Time* CD

Publisher: Jostens Home Learning

Students become familiar with and enjoy classic nursery rhymes in an animated setting. The rhymes are read, and then the students can record their own voices saying the rhymes.

Title: *Richard Scarry's Best Reading Program Ever*

Publisher: Simon & Schuster Interactive

In Busytown, students develop reading-readiness skills, including phonics and story writing. Students can read or hear stories, as well as work with such reading and phonics activities as a clickable dictionary.

Title: *Rudy Reader*

Publisher: Milliken

Rudy the Robot helps students read by teaching them the alphabet on the keyboard, as well as by sight and sound. Students learn beginning and ending sounds. A number of activities are used to teach the different word lists.

LANGUAGE ARTS SOFTWARE *(cont.)*

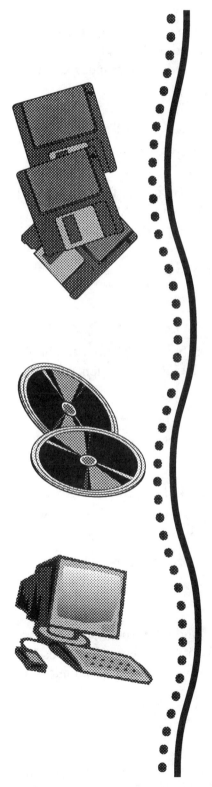

Title: *Ruff's Bone*

Publisher: Brøderbund

Ruff goes on an adventure when he searches for his missing bone and then tries to find his way home safely.

Title: *Sesame Street*

Publisher: Creative Wonders

Students join the cast of Sesame Street to learn important kindergarten and first grade concepts.

- — Art Workshop
- — Elmo's Preschool
- — Get Set to Learn
- — Let's Make a Word
- — Letters
- — Numbers

Title: *Sheila Rae, the Brave*

Publisher: Brøderbund

Based on the book by Kevin Henkes, Sheila Rae is afraid of nothing. Yet when she loses her way, it is her timid little sister who finds the way home. Included are a Map Game and a Sing Along activity.

Title: *Sitting on the Farm*

Publisher: Sanctuary Woods

An interactive, animated story includes engaging skill-building language arts and writing activities. This program is multilingual–English, Spanish, and French.

Title: *SnapDragon*

Publisher: MECC

Students join a camera-happy dragon and his teddy bear as they explore the concepts of classification and grouping with animation and sound effects.

LANGUAGE ARTS SOFTWARE *(cont.)*

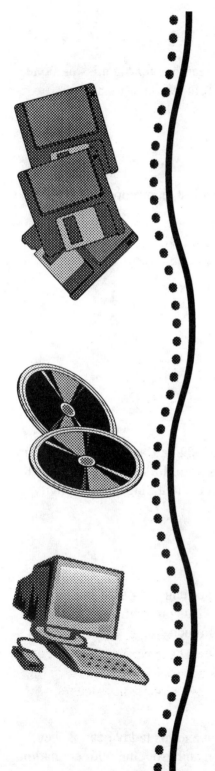

Title: *Snoopy's Campfire Stories*

Publisher: Virgin Sound and Vision

Featuring original television animation and character voices, this program lets students sharpen reading and writing skills by interacting with the Peanuts gang. This program includes six stories and interactive letter-writing activities.

Title: *Stanley's Sticker Stories*

Publisher: Edmark

Millie, Bailey, Sammy, and Trudy, characters from the Edmark early childhood series, can be placed in their own animated storybooks, building reading and spelling skills and expanding creativity.

Title: *Stellaluna*

Publisher: Brøderbund

Based on Janell O'Connell's best-selling book about a young fruit bat, the 14 interactive pages develop early learning skills and build excitement about the joys of reading. Included is a science section with facts about bats and their world.

Title: *Stickybear's Early Learning*

Publisher: Optimum Resource

This award-winning program promotes skill building with six activities: Alphabet, Counting, Grouping, Shapes, Opposites, and Colors. This program is bilingual–English and Spanish.

Title: *Stickybear's Reading Fun Park*

Publisher: Optimum Resource

The famous Stickbeary family guides students through unique, action-packed activities with hundreds of high-frequency words. The activities build sight vocabulary and provide practice in phonics, reading, and memory.

Title: *Stickybear's Reading Room*

Publisher: Optimum Resource

Word Bop, Word Find, Sentence Builder, and Word Match are the activities that provide reading and thinking skill building in Spanish or English. As students create sentences, they are read back to them.

LANGUAGE ARTS SOFTWARE *(cont.)*

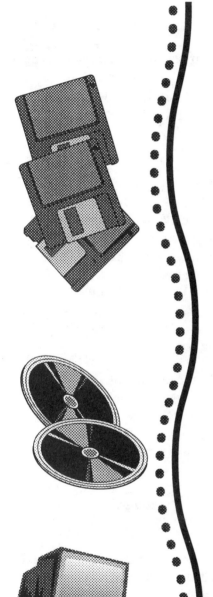

Title: *Storybook Maker* CD

Publisher: Hartley

Young learners create their own stories filled with graphics, objects, and sounds. A variety of settings and hundreds of picture cards of animals, people, places, and objects allow children to create an unlimited number of unique stories.

Title: *Storybook Weaver*

Publisher: MECC

Music, graphics, sounds, and text all can be combined for producing a product ready to publish. Stories can be published and also read aloud to the writers. It is also available in a Spanish version.

Title: *Talking First Words*

Publisher: Orange Cherry/New Media

This five-part program to help students recognize and create words includes Talking Noun Board, Action Blocks, Word Machine, What Am I, and Sentence Fun to provide vehicles for learning in this spoken language program.

Title: *Tortoise and the Hare*

Publisher: Brøderbund

A retelling of Aesop's Fable with new twists keeps the story fresh through clickable hot spots and focused text.

Title: *The Ultimate Writing and Creativity Center*

Publisher: The Learning Company

Specific writing needs for students are addressed, including creativity and editing. The five stages of the writing process are addressed specifically, including a presentation theater for sharing work with others. Students can produce reports, newsletters, storybooks, and signs. Four lands provide writing ideas, and a picture place lets students paint their own pictures or add clip art, photos, sound, music, and animation.

LANGUAGE ARTS SOFTWARE *(cont.)*

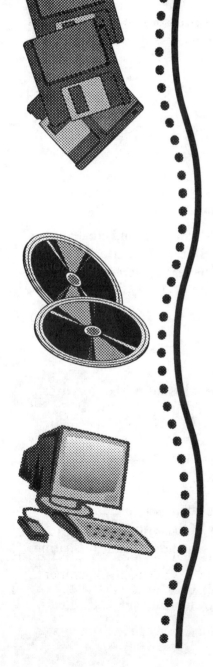

Title: *Words Around Me*

Publisher: Edmark

A step-by-step process for learning common vocabulary words in both English and Spanish is provided. This software divides 275 words and plurals into common sets of about 40 words. Several photographs and illustrations portray each word.

Title: *Word Gallery Series*

Publisher: EPC

Flash Cards, Word Match, Missing Letter, Word Guess, and Word Spell are the activities that are used in thematic modules including home, animals, survival words, school time, and me and mine to teach word recognition and object association.

Title: *Word Munchers*

Publisher: MECC

Students are helped to master the skill of recognizing and distinguishing target vowel sounds by racing a Muncher through a grid, gobbling up appropriate words. Three levels of play and a practice feature allow students to use the maze and word lists without the added challenge of the Troggles.

Title: *Word Stuff: A Multimedia Picture Dictionary*

Publisher: Sanctuary Woods

Over 170 words are defined through graphics and sound. Students can record their own voices and print dictionary books. This program is bilingual–English and Spanish.

Title: *Zurk's Learning Safari*

Publisher: Soleil Software

Students explore the Serengeti where letters of the alphabet morph into animals. Seven games teach learning skills including math, science and prereading.

MATH SOFTWARE

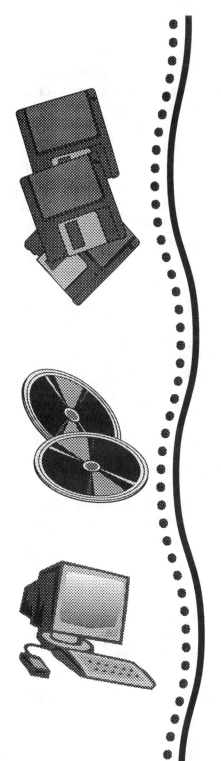

Title: *Bit-Bot's Math Voyage*

Publisher: Sanctuary Woods

Nine activities in four levels of difficulty for students are in this math game with a submarine theme.

Title: *Blocks in Motion*

Publisher: Don Johnston

Based on the Piagetian theory for motor-sensory development, this program promotes the concept that the process is as educational as the end result. Students practice with on-screen manipulatives.

Title: *Clock Shop*

Publisher: Nordic

Teaching digital and analog time by using multiple lesson options and skill levels, it also includes the ability to print work sheets.

Title: *Coin Critters*

Publisher: Nordic

Students develop an understanding of money by learning the face value of coins, purchasing, matching, and counting back change on several levels of difficulty.

Title: *Early Munchers*

Publisher: MECC

Graphics, animation, math, and sound provide positive reinforcement to build confidence in early reading, math, and thinking skills. Included are numbers, patterns, counting, shapes, time, and money.

Title: *Hands-On Math I, II, III*

Publisher: Ventura Educational Systems

This series simulates the use of manipulatives such as colored rods, tiles, counters, chip trading, geoboards, and tangrams on screen. The Playground section of the program allows students to experiment with mathematical ideas. Hands on Math II simulates the use of two-color counters, color tiles, mirrors, attribute blocks, and base-ten blocks. Math III simulates the use of hundreds charts, graphing activities, number balance, dominoes, aesthenometry, and fraction bars.

MATH SOFTWARE *(cont.)*

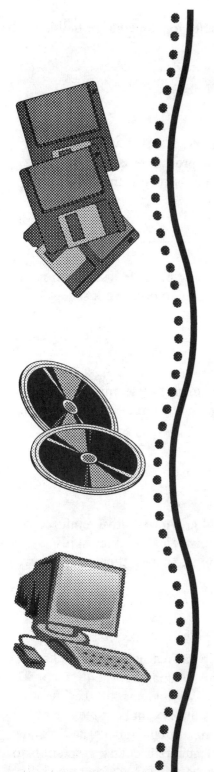

Title: *How Many Bugs in a Box?*

Publisher: Simon & Schuster

David Carter's book is used as a base in this interactive program where students explore eight math learning games, each with three levels. The music and sound effects are enchanting.

Title: *Interactive Math Journey*

Publisher: The Learning Company

Teaching math concepts as well as providing math facts drills, there are 25 carefully sequenced activities. The three-step approach combines the best of exploration exercises with traditional skill-building activities.

Title: *KidsMath*

Publisher: Great Wave

Included are eight activities to teach and reinforce basic math concepts along with introducing 18 different skills.

Title: *Madeline's Thinking Games*

Publisher: Creative Wonders

Games and puzzles exist in every room of Madeline's Parisian mansion. Covered are memory and logical thinking, beginning French and Spanish vocabulary, problem solving and following directions, and music patterning and composition.

Title: *Magic Applehouse*

Publisher: Thomson Learning Tools

This interactive program helps students learn databases, spreadsheets, and business awareness as they help Abigail run her apple business. Included are writing and math activities.

Title: *Math Blaster 1: In Search of Spot*

Publisher: Davidson and Associates

A video arcade-style math facts game, success in the mission to rescue Spot is a joint function of math ability and hand-eye-mouse coordination.

MATH SOFTWARE *(cont.)*

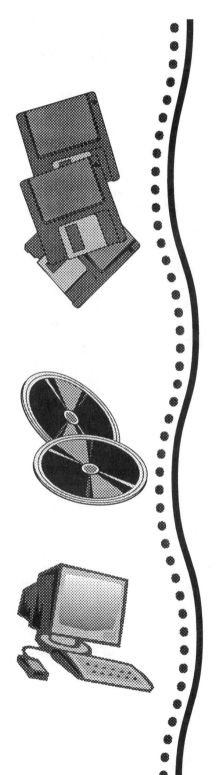

Title: *Math Keys*

Publisher: MECC

This English and Spanish software series links manipulatives, symbolic notation, and writing tools in a learning environment that encourages students to think and communicate mathematically with the aid of on-screen manipulatives. Whole Numbers K-2, Probability K-2, and Geometry K-2 are available.

Title: *Math Magic*

Publisher: Mindplay

Students fight off monsters while they answer elementary math questions. They start with counting objects and progress to addition and subtraction. Records are kept automatically.

Title: *Math Rabbit*

Publisher: The Learning Company

Four different games set at a circus deal with counting, matching, and simple addition and subtraction. Students should be able to count and recognize numbers before using Math Rabbit.

Title: *Math Shop Jr.*

Publisher: Scholastic

Students use everyday math while working in a mall for early development of addition, subtraction, odd/even numbers, estimation, and more.

Title: *Math Splash*

Publisher: Optimum Resource

An unlimited number of math problems cover addition, subtraction, multiplication, and division along with dozens of ways to practice these skills, all in an environment of pirates, sharks, boats, and submarines.

Title: *Mathville 1, 2, 3*

Publisher: Didatech

A computer simulated village where students use their math skills to solve problems of everyday life, emphasis is on second grade skills. This is a practice and reinforcement program.

MATH SOFTWARE *(cont.)*

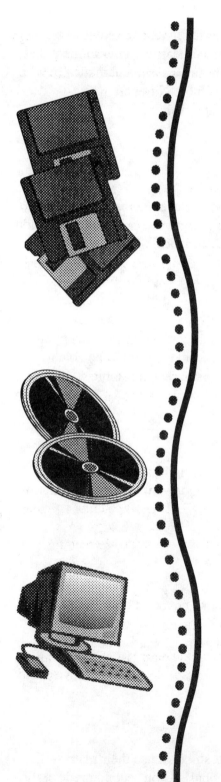

Title: *Math Workshop*

Publisher: Brøderbund

Students practice critical math skills with games, music, animated characters and more. Students build problem solving, strategy, and computational skills.

Title: *Mighty Math Carnival Countdown*

Publisher: Edmark

Students are led through a fairground where they learn about logic and number sets in a bumper-car course. Place values—ones, tens, hundreds, and how place is influenced by addition and subtraction— are explored by blowing bubbles of different sizes.

Title: *Millie's Math House*

Publisher: Edmark

Students explore addition, subtraction, and counting from 1–30, as well as shapes and patterns in six interactive activities.

Title: *Money Town*

Publisher: Simon & Schuster—Davidson and Associates

Five activities help students learn about earning, saving, making change, coin recognition, and more—based on the *The Kid's Money Book* by Neale Godrey.

Title: *More Bugs in Boxes*

Publisher: Simon & Schuster

Based on David Carter's book, this program strengthens basic skills such as color/pattern discrimination, comparing/contrasting attributes, visual/musical memory, logic, and reasoning. The music stays in your head for days.

Title: *Number Maze Challenge*

Publisher: Great Wave Software

Children use three-dimensional mazes as the vehicle for solving math problems. The program tracks children's progress, uses frequent rewards, and a text-to-speech capability for word problems. Animated tutorials introduce and review concepts. Number Maze on disc has multiple levels and keeps records.

MATH SOFTWARE *(cont.)*

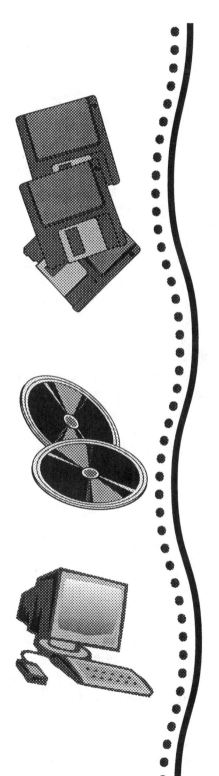

Title: *Snootz Math Trek* CD

Publisher: Theatrix Interactive

Through five playful activities, students discover solutions to a range of mathematical thinking problems including sequencing, map reading, cause and effect, geometric shapes, spatial visualization, symbols and codes, and more.

Title: *Stickybear's Math Town*

Publisher: Optimum Resource

Students choose one of several really unique locations as the backdrop for math problems and real-life word problems. Included are six transparent levels of difficulty involving problems with addition, subtraction, multiplication, and division—plus multiple operations for solving word problems. Providing verbal and visual reinforcement this program is bilingual in English and Spanish.

Title: *Talking Clock*

Publisher: Heartsoft

A friendly human voice guides students while they learn counting and time-telling skills. Students learn to set and tell time on both conventional and digital clocks.

Title: *Thinking Things Collection 1*

Publisher: Edmark

Students are asked to make logical comparisons, deductions, repeat and improvise, and experiment with partial relationships. All questions and instructions are graphical or spoken—no reading is required.

Title: *Thinking Things Collection 2*

Publisher: Edmark

The five activities challenge students to develop problem-solving skills, memory skills, visual thinking, listening skills, creativity, and much more.

Title: *Tommy the Time Turtle*

Publisher: Heartsoft

Students are walked through the process of telling time on a conventional clock face by Tommy the animated turtle. It also comes in a Spanish version.

MATH SOFTWARE *(cont.)*

Title: *Treasure Galaxy*

Publisher: The Learning Company

Students use critical thinking skills and everyday math concepts to solve problems in a highly animated environment.

Title: *Treasure MathStorm*

Publisher: The Learning Company

An alpine adventure game challenges students to apply real-life math and thinking skills such as counting money, making change, and reading clocks. Students also practice place value, number sequences, and equalities and inequalities on six math levels.

Title: *Trudy's Time and Place House*

Publisher: Edmark

In five activities, students explore geography and time. Students learn time-telling skills using talking clocks and explore the concept of time by fast forwarding and rewinding an animated movie by seconds, minutes, hours, days, and months. Students also discover the relationships among earth, globe, and atlas, identify continents and ocean, and develop mapping and direction skills.

Title: *Turbo Math Facts*

Publisher: Nordic Software

Students practice addition, subtraction, multiplication, and division in the pursuit of money to buy the fastest car.

Title: *Zoo Zillions*

Publisher: Edmark

Word problems and money concepts in a safari setting entice students. An aquarium with various kinds of fish is filled by students who answer questions about a story and make change for animal customers in the Gnu Ewe Boutique.

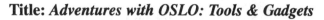

SCIENCE SOFTWARE

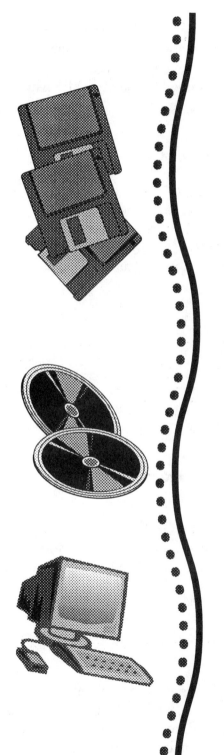

Title: *Adventures with OSLO: Tools & Gadgets*

Publisher: Science for Kids

This physical science program explores simple machines and combines education with entertainment for students as they learn through an animated storybook. It covers all six classes of simple machines—the inclined plane, screw, pulley, wheel and axle, and lever and wedge.

Title: *Animal Kingdom*

Publisher: Unicorn

Students are introduced to the wonders of the animal kingdom and various zoological species with learning games which build reading, memory, and discrimination skills.

Title: *Backyard*

Publisher: Brøderbund

Animal habitats, caterpillar life cycles, mapping, and directional skills are introduced to students.

Title: *Body Park*

Publisher: Virtual Entertainment

Albert and friends provide a fun and educational way for students to learn about anatomy, nutrition, and general health and safety within an exciting theme park complete with rides, games, and all sorts of attractions.

Title: *Bumptz Science Carnival* CD

Publisher: Theatrix

Students become scientific thinkers as they join Bumptz on a field trip to the Great Galaxies Amusement Park. Over 200 animated puzzles with three skill levels are included as students play with the properties of light, buoyancy, and magnetism. A construction kit which lets kids create their own science puzzles includes 12 animated movie shorts about how science works on Earth and 20 hands-on experiments students can do at home.

SCIENCE SOFTWARE *(cont.)*

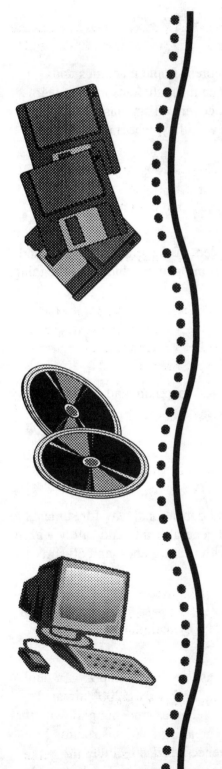

Title: *"Cell"ebration!* CD

Publisher: Science for Kids

The interactive CD-ROM lessons and hands-on lab materials pique students' curiosity with views of the cells while they learn the differences between living and nonliving things, characteristics of living organisms, processes of maintaining life and organelles, and the nature of cell structure.

Title: *Explorapedia: The World of Nature* CD

Publisher: Microsoft

Students learn about rain forests, polar regions, lakes, deserts, oceans, grasslands, mountains, savannas, deciduous forests, and more. Included are more than 200 topics, over 50 videos, an hour of intriguing animation, original songs, and more than 400 sounds.

Title: *How Animals Move*

Publisher: Discovery Communications

Narrated tours take students flying, crawling, jumping, and more with over 250 videos of animals in motion. Students can create their own animals and see how they move. The program prints and parts can be copied to productivity programs.

Title: *Imagination Express: Destination RainForest*

Publisher: Edmark

Students interact with exotic plants and animals, interesting characters, and lush sights and sounds to create interactive stories set in the rain forest. Students select scenes and add clip art, text, sound effects, dialog, and narration to publish their creations.

Title: *Imagination Express: Destination Ocean*

Publisher: Edmark

Students create their own interactive stories by incorporating beautiful backgrounds, realistic clip art, sound, and motion. There is also a fact book of information that students use in creating their stories. Students learn about ocean habitats, the role of oceans in ecosystems, and more.

SCIENCE SOFTWARE *(cont.)*

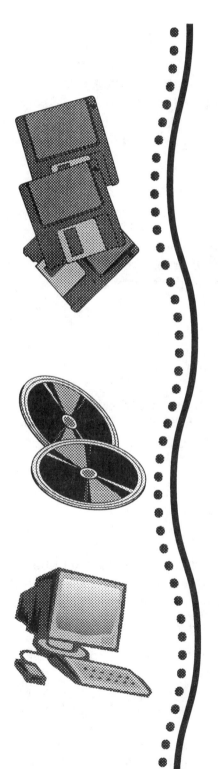

Title: *Jungle Safari*

Publisher: Talking Schoolhouse

Eighty animals and plants in a multisensory tour of four habitats are presented in this program. Full-color graphics, sound effects, and narration make the safari complete.

Title: *Learning About Animals*

Publisher: Talking Schoolhouse

Students learn how animals are classified according to group and species. They see how variations in animal bodies and behavior enable them to adapt to various habitats and climates.

Title: *Magic School Bus Explores Inside the Earth*

Publisher: Microsoft

Students explore six geological zones (canyon, underwater volcano, giant fault, deep cavern, land volcano, and a forming geode) to discover clues in the search to find missing rocks and minerals. There are four different interactive experiments.

Title: *Magic School Bus Explores the Human Body*

Publisher: Microsoft

Arnold's body is explored from inside the school bus. Along the way explorations are made into how the human body works.

Title: *Magic School Bus Explores the Oceans*

Publisher: Microsoft

Students explore seven ocean zones and solve the clues to find the sunken treasure. With special underwater diving gear, students can swim around and explore the plants, fish, mammals, and other creature and plants.

Title: *Magic School Bus Explores the Solar System*

Publisher: Microsoft

Students discover the secrets of the solar system and win the game when they collect the clues. Three-dimensional forms are used in the investigation of the solar system.

SCIENCE SOFTWARE *(cont.)*

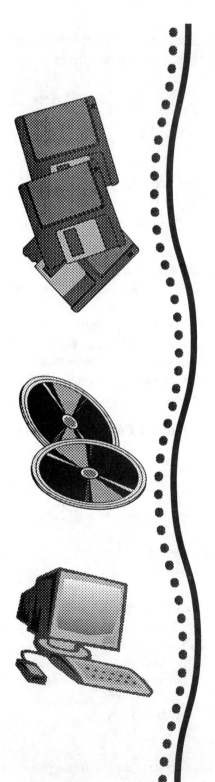

Title: *Mammals: A Multimedia Encyclopedia* **CD**

Publisher: National Geographic

More then 200 mammals are included on this CD-ROM. Video clips, sound, photographs, fact boxes, and range maps are included, plus the equivalent of 600 pages of text. Also included are a narrated tutorial, glossary terms, a classification game, and printing capability.

Title: *Multimedia Bird Book*

Publisher: Expert Software

Students go on a photojournalism assignment and search for information for a bird magazine. They travel through seven animated habitats, witnessing the living habits of birds and learning to identify them.

Title: *Multimedia Bug Book*

Publisher: Expert Software

Dr. Anson Pzntz's bug collection has escaped, and he needs help to retrieve them. There are five different habitats to explore. Clicking on the bug captures it and provides video clips, sounds, and pictures of bugs in action.

Title: *One Small Square: Backyard*

Publisher: Virgin Sound and Vision

Using software based on the acclaimed Scientific American Books for young Readers Series, students explore 60 natural environments in a three-dimensional setting. They access data on backyard plants and animals and can conduct twelve different experiments and log and print the results in a journal.

Title: *One Small Square: Seashore*

Publisher: Virgin Sound and Vision

One small square of a seashore's ecosystem is explored by students with in-depth information on over 170 plants and animals through 115 videos and animated sequences.

SCIENCE SOFTWARE *(cont.)*

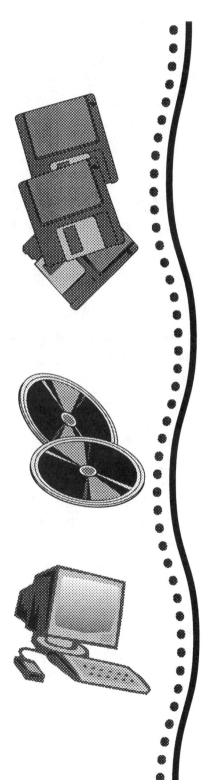

Title: *Ozzie's World* CD

Publisher: Digital Impact

Students join Ozzie Otter on an animated, earth-friendly exploration through the world of science. They tour five environments where animals talk and share their stories and where puzzles, games, and coloring books are hidden around every corner.

Title: *Plants* CD

Publisher: Clearvue

This new interactive program emphasizes the biosphere as a web of interrelationships and examines plants as a basic and integral part of human and animal life. Topics include plants, plant food, flowers, and trees.

Title: Putt-Putt Saves the Zoo

Publisher: Humongous Entertainment

Putt-Putt discovers the zoo animals are missing and solves puzzles to find them. Habitats Laser DiscSVE shows how animals make their homes, how they live in land, sea, water, and air. Live photography is used.

Title: *Sammy's Science House*

Publisher: Edmark

Students practice observing, sorting, comparing, and sequencing as they explore fundamental scientific processes in two levels of involvement. The teacher materials are superior in this product.

Title: *The San Diego Zoo Presents The Animals! 2.0*

Publisher: Mindscape

Two hundred exotic mammals, birds, and reptiles in their natural surroundings provide reference materials for students to use in research. Movies, sounds, and stories make it fun and easy for students. With over 60 minutes of motion video, 1,300 color photos, and 1,000 pages of animal data, narrated tours guide students through exciting areas such as animals in disguise, jaws, claws, and creature features.

SCIENCE SOFTWARE *(cont.)*

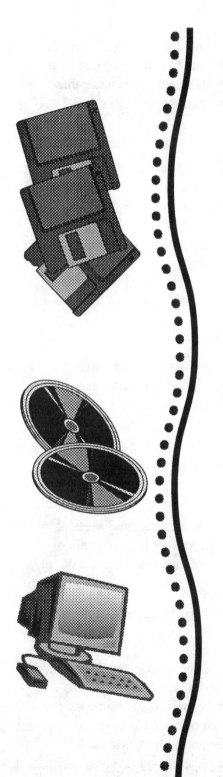

Title: *Science Blaster Jr.*

Publisher: Davidson & Associates

This program highlights progressively challenging steps that build essential logic and thinking skills. There are 30 printable experiments that students can do at home. Students learn about weather, seasons, properties of animals, plants, and the world around them.

Title: *Super Solvers Gizmos & Gadgets!*

Publisher: The Learning Company

Over 200 puzzles and simulations help students understand physical science concepts such as magnetism, electricity, balance, force, and gravity.

Title: *Zoo Keeper*

Publisher: Davidson and Associates

To maintain zookeeper status, students must keep the animals happy by learning about environments and foods suited for particular animals.

Title: *Zoo-Opolis!*

Publisher: Compton's New Media

Students journey into the colorful world of Zoo-Opolis where they learn about animals, zoos and the environment while reinforcing their reading, memory, computation, and puzzle skills. Featured are award-winning video footage plus game shows, zookeepers, and a Zoo TV.

Title: *Zootopia*

Publisher: Publisher: Lawrence Productions

As students journey through the zoo, they encounter animals that sing the blues, listen to Lion's talk radio show, or even buy a used camel at "Camel Lot."

Title: *Zurk's Rainforest Lab*

Publisher: Soliel

Early readers are exposed to life science and math, using the rain forest as a classroom. Five fun and challenging activities use picture-book-quality, true-to-like graphics and accurate animations of 50 animals to teach students. English, French, and Spanish languages are available.

SOCIAL STUDIES SOFTWARE

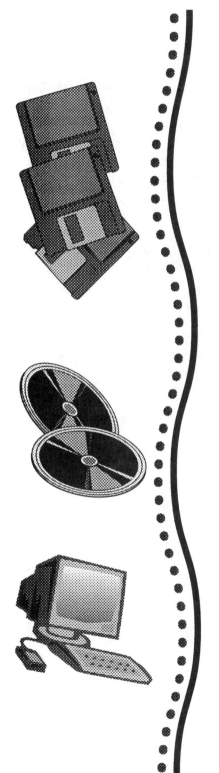

Title: *Choices, Choices*

Publisher: Tom Snyder Productions

Students face choices every day, and this program provides young students with the skills and awareness they need to set goals, make predictions, and face the consequences of their actions. The three topics are On the Playground, Taking Responsibility, and Kids and the Environment.

Title: *Imagination Express: Neighborhood*

Publisher: Edmark

This creative program allows students to write and choose clip art for their illustrations from a thematic base of graphics related to their neighborhood: the park, the school, a secret fort, and other familiar places. Students combine text, music, sounds, dialog, and narration to write about their daily adventures.

Title: *Let's Explore the Airport with Buzzy* CD

Publisher: Humongous

Students visit an airport and see the ticket counter, controls in the cockpit of the Concorde, and how the ground crew prepares the planes. They also go behind the scenes to see where the baggage goes.

Title: *Richard Scarry's How Things Work in Busytown*

Publisher: Simon & Schuster Interactive

Students explore the nature and importance of jobs in a town through the wonderful drawings of Richard Scarry. Covered are the farm, the mill, the assembly plant, building the road, the garbage truck, the recycling plant, and the toy factory.

Title: *TimeLiner*

Publisher: Tom Snyder Productions

Creating time lines in any subject area is simple with this multiaged program. Teachers and students can create time lines for a day, a week, a month, or longer periods with this program.

SOCIAL STUDIES SOFTWARE *(cont.)*

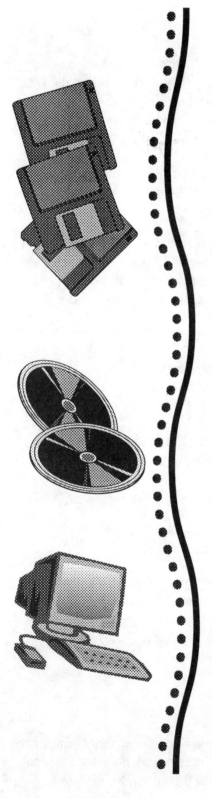

Title: *Trudy's Time and Place House*

Publisher: Edmark

Students explore geography and time. They discover the relationship among the earth, globe, and atlas, identify continents and oceans, and develop mapping and direction skills.

Title: *Where in the World is Carmen Sandiego? Jr. Detective Edition*

Publisher: Brøderbund

Providing a basic introduction to world geography, it focuses on individual geographic regions and countries around the world. Visual clues are used by the students to track down the elusive Carmen.

REFERENCE SOFTWARE

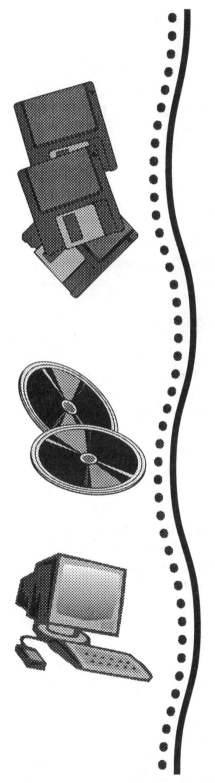

Title: *American Heritage Children's Dictionary* CD

Publisher: Houghton Mifflin Interactive

A true multimedia dictionary created for today's students, it incorporates the complete text of the updated third edition of the dictionary and is packed with thousands of pictures, lively sounds, and whimsical animation that bring words to life.

Title: *Children's Atlas of the United States* CD

Publisher: Rand McNally

Students get an informative and entertaining look at the United States. Featured are animated markers that show state capitals, largest cities, rivers and mountains, graphs, cards, and more for each state and the District of Columbia along with six games.

Title: *Children's World Atlas* CD

Publisher: Rand McNally

Eight video clips, photographs, graphs, and fully narrated descriptions keep students actively involved in exploring the world through an atlas. Included are six educational games from around the world.

Title: *First Connections: The Golden Book Encyclopedia* CD

Publisher: Hartley

More than 1,500 articles and 2,700 color images are all designed to engage students in an interactive learning experience. Online audio instructions explain what's on the screen. A built-in notebook allows students to take notes.

Title: *Macmillan Dictionary for Children* CD

Publisher: Simon & Schuster Interactive

Audio in three languages helps students use this visual dictionary. Graphics, animation, sound, and interactivity make this a unique reference work which contains over 3,000 entries and over 3,500 color images.

REFERENCE SOFTWARE *(cont.)*

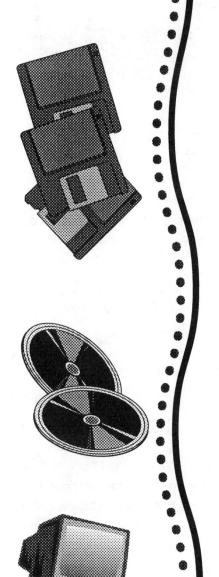

Title: *Microsoft Explorapedia: The World of People*

Publisher: Microsoft

Through content, sound, and animation, students discover a wealth of information pertaining to people and what they do in the fields of science, art, literature, transportation, theater, sports, farming, and more. Students are guided through more than 180 topics. For early or prereaders, content can be narrated.

Title: *My First Incredible Amazing Dictionary*

Publisher: DK Multimedia

Containing 17,000 words, 1,000 of which have definitions, it has 1000 illustrations and animations. This dictionary also contains three interactive games which help students learn about words.

Title: *Talking Encyclopedia for Children* **CD**

Publisher: SoftBit

More than 1,000 pages of text, 1,700 illustrations, and 12 hours of audio take students on a narrative tour through topics ranging from dinosaurs to Plymouth Rock. Categories include biology, astronomy, geography, nature, and more.

Title: *Ultimate Children's Encyclopedia*

Publisher: The Learning Company

Using a complete reference library that includes dictionary, thesaurus, atlas, biographies, and a book of words, students start a search by clicking on objects which represent categories: science, machines, or countries, for example. Within each category are hundreds of topics presented through photos, articles, maps, time lines, and videos.

Title: *The Way Things Work* **CD**

Publisher: DK Multimedia

Animation, audio and wonderful illustrations help students learn about the greatest scientific discoveries from 7,000 B.C. to the present. The new version connects to the Internet where there is a site dedicated to information related to the CD-ROM.

CREATIVITY SOFTWARE *(cont.)*

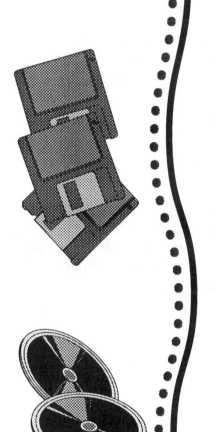

Title: *Amazing Animation* CD

Publisher: Claris

Students can create interactive multimedia stories, poems, reports and movies. They can also produce computer animations with animated characters, realistic sounds, and special effects.

Title: *Delta Drawing Today*

Publisher: Power Industries

Based on learning through graphic manipulation, students create original artwork that reinforces basic curriculum objectives.

Title: *Incredible Coloring Kit*

Publisher: Creative Pursuits

Students create their own coloring books in any of nine themes. They combine colors, designs, stickers, and words to create their own pictures. It prints in several sizes.

Title: *Kid Riffs*

Publisher: IBM Software

Making music is easy as students experience the fun of creating and recording new tunes or playing along with prerecorded musical riffs. They experiment with many instruments in the Instrument Inn, learn about scales on the Musical Stairway, and set up rhythms and intervals on the Clickit Fence.

Title: *Kid Pix Studio*

Publisher: Brøderbund

This CD-ROM enhanced version of *Kid Pix* has added new features including animation. With over 100 video clips, songs, and sound effects, it contains 14 different fonts and more than 800 stamps, plus photo CD support capability.

CREATIVITY SOFTWARE *(cont.)*

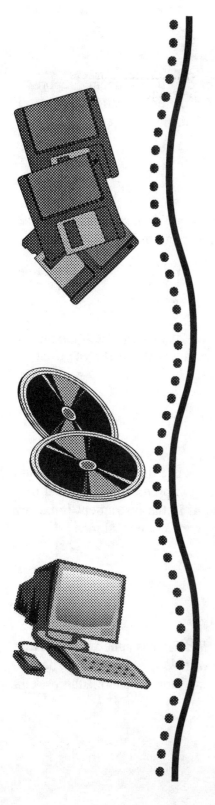

Title: *The New Kid Pix*

Publisher: Brøderbund

A paint and writing program with graphics, sounds and recording capabilities, this is great for teachers and students to use to create slide shows. Included are hundreds of rubber stamps which can be customized, screen transitions, paintbrushes, and a slide show feature for creation of multimedia presentations.

Title: *With Open Eyes* **CD**

Publisher: Voyager

Full-screen pictures of over 200 works of art from The Art Institute of Chicago's collection are accompanied by audio clips. Access the collection by geography or time period or view in an automated slide show. Any object can be seen in a virtual gallery.

TEACHER UTILITY SOFTWARE

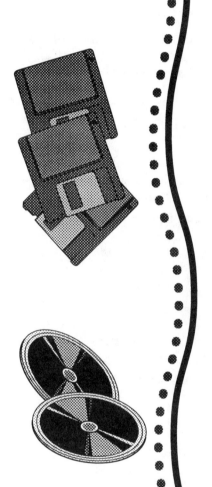

Title: *Award Maker Plus*

Publisher: Baudville

Make professional-quality certificates with detailed borders, specialized graphics, and personalized messages.

Title: *BannerMania*

Publisher: Broderbund

To produce banners, posters, and bumper stickers, choose from 19 fonts and 27 different shapes from convex to kinky ribbon and from shadow to perspective. It prints in black and white or color.

Title: *Friday Afternoon*

Publisher: Hartley

Create bingo games, word searches, worksheets, crossword puzzles, or flashcards from word lists. It handles an unlimited number of word lists.

Title: *Make-a-Flash*

Publisher: Teacher Support Software

Print vocabulary and math flash cards. Enter your own database or import text files.

Title: *Math Companion*

Publisher: Visions Software

Create your own math worksheets in any computational level along with word problem activity sheets. There are over 100 difficulty levels and tutorials with remediation.

Title: *Print Artist 3.0*

Publisher: Sierra

Print posters, signs, greeting cards, banners, stationery, envelopes, and more. Included are professional-quality clip art and over 500 layouts.

TEACHER UTILITY SOFTWARE *(cont.)*

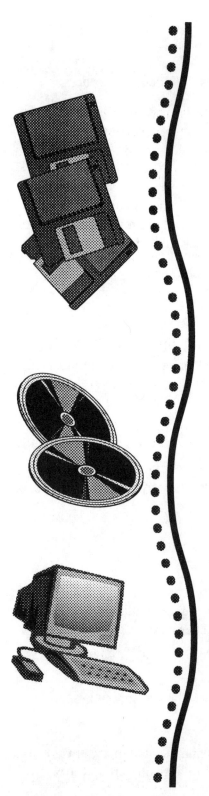

Title: *Printmaster Gold*

Publisher: Mindscape

This CD includes 4500 graphics, 201 fonts, and thousands of special text effects for any print projects that you need to do quickly and easily.

Title: *Print Pizazz*

Publisher: Creative Pursuits

Create school-printed materials with an array of over 1,000 design elements including school fonts, headline fonts, dingbats, line art, borders, ornaments, and certificates. Use it with your favorite word processor.

Title: *The Print Shop Deluxe*

Publisher: Brøderbund

Combine graphics and text to create calendars, banners, newsletters, subject worksheets, bookmarks, greeting cards, and more. Graphics can be exported for use in other programs, and certain graphic formats can be imported.

Title: *Teacher Helper Plus*

Publisher: Visions Software

An easy-to-use program for creating worksheets and tests, it includes multiple choice, true/false, word-search puzzle, matching, and fill-in blanks. Instant access to unlimited graphics along with 100 original graphics are included.

Title: *Teacher Tool Kit*

Publisher: Hi-Tech of Santa Cruz

Design curriculum-based activities for any subject or grade level. Included are word searches, scrambles, matching and multiple choice for unlimited puzzles or tests.

GLOSSARY

A

Adapter—electronic piece that adapts to a device so a computer can control the device.

After Dark—a utility from Berkeley Systems called a screen saver.

AppleTalk—the AppleTalk network is how your Mac talks to your laser printer, other Macs, or other machines. All these machines need to be hooked up in order to talk.

Application—a computer software program you use.

B

Bar code—grouping of thin lines which when accessed by an electronic bar-code reader, reveal information.

Baud (baud rate)—speed that a MODEM can send information.

Bit—short for binary digit. One bit is the smallest unit of information that the computer can work with.

Bulletin Board Service—service usually set up by an online organization to provide or exchange information.

Bundling—usually, the practice of selling hardware (e.g., a computer) and including free one or more pieces of software.

Button—electronic item on a computer screen that is "pushed" in order for something to happen.

Byte—a byte is eight bits strung together. Most computer information is organized into bytes.

C

CD-ROM—compact disk read-only memory. A disc which holds up to 600 megabytes of information.

CD-ROM Player—disk drive which allows the CD-ROM to be played.

Clip Art—artwork that is electronically cut and pasted onto other documents.

CPU—central processing unit. The "brains" of a computer. Often a tiny microprocessor chip which runs the entire system.

Crash—what happens when your computer stops working suddenly or the system breaks down. (A very bad deal!)

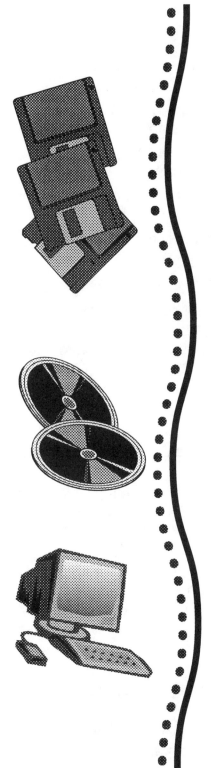

GLOSSARY *(cont.)*

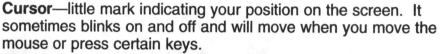

Cursor—little mark indicating your position on the screen. It sometimes blinks on and off and will move when you move the mouse or press certain keys.

D

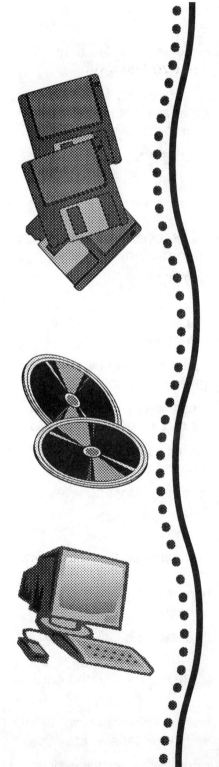

Database—collection of information stored in computerized form.

Default—any time an automatic decision is already made for you by the computer or software program.

Desktop—background on your screen when you are using a Macintosh, or other windows-like program.

Desktop Publishing—process of creating printed documents that look professionally produced.

Dialog Box—a box or window on the screen that you can "dialog" with and make choices from.

Digital—information represented by numbers.

Digital Camera—outputs images in digital form instead of regular photographic film.

Disk—thin, circular, or rectangular object used to store computer data on.

Disk Drive—part of the computer where the disk goes.

DOS—disk operating systems. Many types of computers have systems called DOS. Usually refers to IBM PC or other compatible computers.

Download—to receive information (like a file) from another computer to yours through the MODEM. Or you may take a copy of a document from a disk and download it onto your computer.

Drag—use the mouse to position the pointer over an object, press and hold the mouse button and move the mouse, thereby moving the object to another position on the screen.

E

E-mail—short for electronic mail you can send or receive directly on your computer via MODEM.

Ethernet—a local area network connecting computers together with cables so the computers can share the same information.

GLOSSARY *(cont.)*

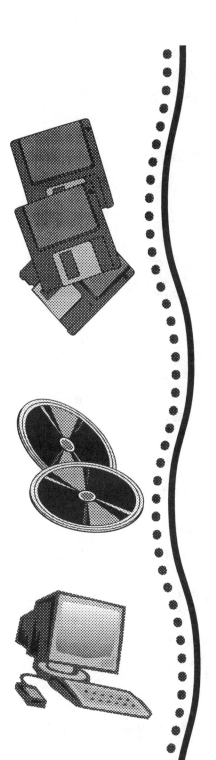

F

Fiber Optics—a communications system that uses dozens of hair-thin strands of glass that move information at the speed of light.

Font—a complete set of type of one size and style.

G

Graphic—an electronic picture.

H

Hacker—computer enthusiast who is willing to "hack" away at understanding the computer for long periods of time.

Hardware—parts of the computer which are external (MODEM, printer, hard drive, keyboard).

HyperCard/HyperStudio—software applications which use multimedia and are interactive.

I

IBM (International Business Machines)—an international computer company.

Icons—little pictures on the screen which represent files of other computer applications.

Import—to bring information from one document or computer screen into another document.

Interactive—program, game, or presentation where the user has some control over what is going on.

Interface—connection between two items so they can work together.

Internet—worldwide network of about half a million computers belonging to research organizations, the military, institutions of learning, corporations, and so on.

K

K, KB (Kilobyte)—a unit for measuring the size of things on hard disks or computer applications. It represents the memory of an item. One kilobyte is equal to 1,024 bytes.

Keyboard—piece of hardware that has the keys, like a typewriter.

GLOSSARY *(cont.)*

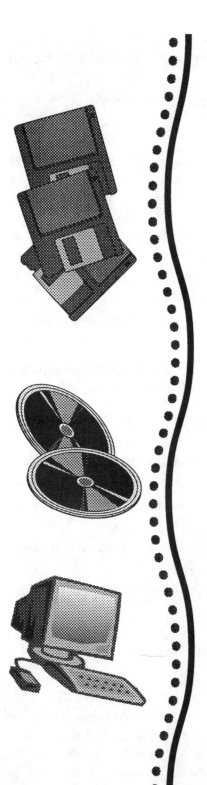

L

Laptop Computer—a computer small enough to fit on your lap. Runs on batteries and is portable.

Laserdisc—also known as videodisc, similar to a music CD, but it also holds visual images. Information can be accessed by remote control or bar code.

Laserdisc Player—machine which plays the laserdisc.

Laser Printer—printer which produces documents that look professionally printed.

LCD Panel—a device which fits over the overhead projector and, when connected to a computer, will project whatever is on the computer screen onto a large viewing screen. LCD means liquid crystal display. A liquid compound is wedged between two grids of electrodes to create an image.

M

Macintosh—name of an Apple computer which was the first computer to use the windows and mouse formats.

Mb, MB (Megabyte)—short for a unit of measure, measuring the size of electronic items (like files and documents). One megabyte is equal to 1,048,567 bytes of memory.

Memory—temporary storage space in your computer as opposed to the permanent storage space on the hard disk. Think of the hard disk as a filing cabinet where everything is stored. Memory is your desk while you are temporarily working on the items inside the filing cabinet.

Menu—a displayed list of commands or options from which you can choose.

Modem—device that allows computers to communicate with other computers via the telephone line.

Monitor—another word for the computer screen.

Mouse—small device (connected to the keyboard) which you move across the top of your desk to manipulate the pointer or cursor on the screen.

Mouse Pad—a small pad on which you can you roll your mouse around. Designed to give you a better grip than a desktop.

MS-DOS (Microsoft Disk Operating System)—this is the most commonly used system for IBM PC and other compatible computers.

GLOSSARY *(cont.)*

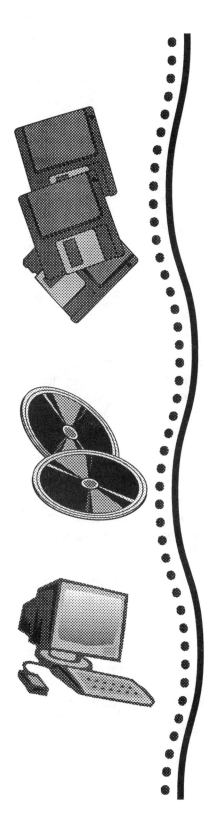

Multimedia—a computer presentation that involves still images, moving video, sound, animation, art, or a combination of all the above.

N

Network—communication or connection system that lets your computer talk with another computer, printer, hard disk, or other device.

O

Online—communicating with other computers through your MODEM or network.

P

Paint Program—software application that provides electronic versions of paintbrushes, paint cans, pencil, eraser, scissors, etc., in order to create illustrations.

PC (Personal Computer)—designed to be used by an individual person.

Port—a socket usually found on the back of hardware where a cable is connected.

PowerBook—Apple's laptop computer.

Printer—device that takes the text and images sent from the computer and presents them on paper.

Prompt—a symbol or question on the screen that "prompts" you to take action and tell the computer what to do next.

Q

QuickTime—software product from Apple that is loaded onto your computer so you can run movies. It requires a great deal of space.

GLOSSARY *(cont.)*

R

RAM (Random Access Memory)—electronic circuits in your computer which hold information. It is the temporary memory used while the computer is turned on. You will need to save any work you do onto a disk or a file on the hard drive. Otherwise, your work will be lost when the computer is shut off. RAM is referred to as volatile because the contents disappear when the computer is turned off.

ROM (Read-Only Memory)—information stored on ROM remains intact. The information is usually programmed right onto the chip or disk and cannot be altered or added to. That is why it is called read-only.

S

Scanner—device that takes a picture of an image that exists outside the computer and digitizes the image to put it on the computer.

Screen Saver—a software application that blanks the screen and replaces the screen with a nonharmful picture. By moving the mouse or touching a key, the screen saver shuts off and your original screen automatically comes back up. if you leave your computer on for a long time, the image can burn onto the screen.

Software—instructions for the computer which are stored on a disk. These disks must be loaded onto the hard drive of the computer so that the computer will know what to do. Some software applications are already loaded onto the computer.

Spreadsheet Program—software program for financial or other number-related information processing. A spreadsheet is composed of rows and columns, with individual boxes (cells) inside of each to hold information.

T

Telecommunications—communications carried on through one computer to another through the telephone and MODEM.

Terminal—a screen and keyboard, along with any circuits necessary to connect it to a main computer.

Toolbox—many software applications, especially ones with paint options, come with a toolbox, which appears on the screen in the form of a palette.

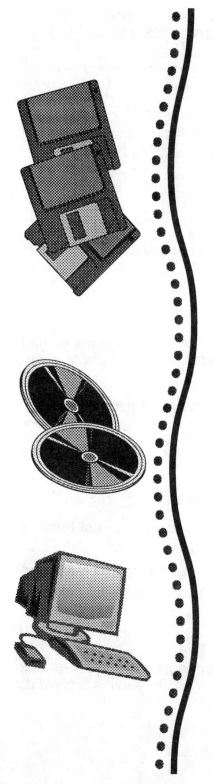

GLOSSARY *(cont.)*

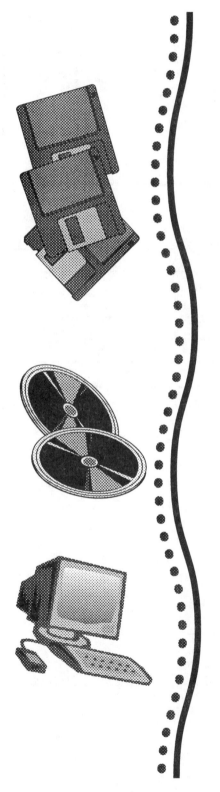

U

Upgrade—to choose newer, more powerful packages (hard or software).

Upload—using a MODEM, you put one of your files onto a network (or online service) and load the file onto the service so other people have access to it.

Utility—a software program that is not used to create something (like an application) but rather it is used to enhance your working environment. After Dark is a utility for your computer system.

V

Videodisc—see laserdisc.

Virus—a software program designed to destroy data on your computer or corrupt your system software. Some viruses are so destructive, they can wipe out entire disks. Viruses are created illegally and can travel from computer to computer through disks, networks, and MODEMs. Using virus detection software is a safe way to protect your system.

Virtual Reality—a simulated environment which appears to be real through use of a computer.

W

Window—rectangular frame on the screen in which you see and work with a particular software application.

Word Processor—software applications that allow you to type documents with a variety of tools to make work time easier and more efficient.

SLIDE SHOW STORYBOARD 1

Slide # _____

Words/Narration _____
_____
_____
_____
_____
_____

Slide # _____

Words/Narration _____
_____
_____
_____
_____
_____

Slide # _____

Words/Narration _____
_____
_____
_____
_____
_____

Slide # _____

Words/Narration _____
_____
_____
_____
_____
_____

SLIDE SHOW STORYBOARD 2

Slide # _____

Slide # _____

Slide # _____

Slide # _____

BIBLIOGRAPHY

Barron, Ann E. and Gary W. Orwig. *New Technologies for Education—A Beginner's Guide.* Libraries Unlimited, 1995.

Bennett, Steve and Ruth. *The Official Kid Pix Activity Book.* Random House, 1993.

Chan, Barbara J. *Kid Pix Around the World—A Multicultural Activity Book.* Addison Wesley, 1993.

Cowan, Bill. *Computer Basics.* Teacher Created Materials, 1995.

Gardner, Paul. *Internet for Teachers and Parents.* Teacher Created Materials, 1996.

Garfield, Gary M. and Suzanne McDonough. *Creating a Technologically Literate Classroom.* Teacher Created Materials, 1995.

Haag, Tim. *Internet for Kids.* Teacher Created Materials, 1996.

Hayes, Deborah. *Managing Technology in the Classroom.* Teacher Created Materials, 1995.

Healey, Deborah. *Something to Do on Tuesday.* Athelstan, 1995.

Lifter, Marsha. *Writing and Desktop Publishing on the Computer* (Primary). Teacher Created Materials, 1996.

Pereira, Linda. *Computers Don't Byte.* Teacher Created Materials, 1996.

Pereira, Linda. *Computers Don't Byte* (Primary). Teacher Created Materials, 1996.

Reidel, Joan. *The Integrated Technology Classroom—Building Self-Reliant Learners.* Allyn & Bacon, 1995.

Willing, Kathleen R. and Suzanne Girard. *Learning Together—Computer Integrated Classrooms.* Pembroke Publishers Ltd., 1990.

Wodaski, Ron. *Absolute Beginner's Guide to Multimedia.* Sams Publishing, 1994.

ONLINE SERVICES

America Online, (800) 827-6364

Classroom PRODIGY Service, (800) 776-3449, ext. 629

CompuServ, (800) 848-8990

Earthlink, (800) 395-8425

Netscape, (415) 254-190